SOCIAL DANCE
INSTRUCTION

Steps to Success

Judy Patterson Wright, PhD
Dance Educator, Champaign, Illinois

Human Kinetics

Library of Congress Cataloging-in-Publication Data

Wright, Judy Patterson, 1946-
    Social dance instruction : steps to success / Judy Patterson Wright.
        p.   cm.—(Steps to success activity series)
    Includes bibliographical references.
    ISBN 0-87322-830-8
    1. Ballroom dancing--Study and teaching. I. Title. II. Series.
GV1751.5.W75   1996
793.'3'3--dc20   95-44481
                                       CIP

ISBN: 0-87322-830-8

Developmental Editor: Rodd Whelpley
Assistant Editor: Kent Reel
Editorial Assistants: Jennifer Hemphill and Alecia Mapes Walk
Copyeditor: David Frattini
Proofreader: Sue Fetters
Typesetter: Kathy Boudreau-Fuoss
Text Design: Keith Blomberg
Text Layout: Denise Lowry
Cover Design: Jack Davis
Cover Photo: Wilmer Zehr
Author Photo: Brian Milhous
Line Drawings: Sharon Barner
Footwork Diagrams: Studio 2D
Mac Artwork: Denise Lowry
Printer: Versa Press

Instructional Designer for the Steps to Success Activity Series: Joan N. Vickers, EdD, University of Calgary, Calgary, Alberta, Canada

Human Kinetics books are available at special discounts for bulk purchase. Special editions or book excerpts can also be created to specification. For details, contact the Special Sales Manager at Human Kinetics.

Printed in the United States of America   10 9 8 7 6 5 4 3 2 1

Human Kinetics
P.O. Box 5076, Champaign, IL 61825-5076
1-800-747-4457

Canada: Human Kinetics, Box 24040, Windsor, ON N8Y 4Y9
1-800-465-7301 (in Canada only)

Europe: Human Kinetics, P.O. Box IW14, Leeds LS16 6TR, United Kingdom
(44) 1132 781708

Australia: Human Kinetics, 2 Ingrid Street, Clapham 5062, South Australia
(08) 371 3755

New Zealand: Human Kinetics, P.O. Box 105-231, Auckland 1
(09) 523 3462

Contents

Preface

Successful social dance instructors analyze skills, understand rhythmic concepts, distinguish different styling techniques, provide feedback, modify experiences for a range of learner skill levels, and effectively manage groups of students. This book provides a systematic way you can become a successful social dance instructor—at a school, at a club, at a community or recreation center, or in a workshop or clinic.

This book is based on the philosophy that people learn progressively through steps that build one upon another. It is an extension of my dissertation results which showed that learners eventually need to integrate both spacial and temporal aspects of their performance, and that teachers can facilitate this learning process by also integrating these aspects when presenting dance moves. Thus, this book introduces not only footwork, but also adds rhythm and timing aspects as well as where to stand and move in relationship to a partner—prior to dancing with a partner. Teaching styles and learning experiences in this book range from the command style to allowing for student problem solving. Mixing effective teaching styles with challenging and fun learning activities (drills) will allow your students the greatest chance to grow. The best way for learning to occur is to share responsibility with your students. Give students some authority to take control of their own learning. Realize that because the participant's book (*Social Dance: Steps to Success*) is a self-paced, individualized approach to social dance, it will complement the shared responsibility approach to teaching. You won't always be with your students when they go dancing, so help them become self-teachers. For example, direct your students to use the sample music (on the soundsheet found in the participant's book) while practicing specific drills for out-of-class assignments. Do not expect your class to go through the learning steps at the same rate. Rather, be aware that you'll need to modify your instructions to fit a range of student skill levels.

Sometimes the difference between social dance and ballroom dance creates confusion. The main difference is in the learner's purpose. *Social dance* in this text refers to using a variety of partner dances (swing, waltz, foxtrot, polka, and cha-cha) to help students dance in a variety of recreational settings—at a school-sponsored dance, at a club, at a park district or community-sponsored dance, at a wedding reception, or at a party. *Ballroom dance* may include the same partner dances as listed previously; however, as the name implies, it is often done in a ballroom setting, or in competition. The latter is a natural extension for those students who want to refine their technique and styling beyond a recreational interest.

This book is especially designed to help those graduate assistants, physical educators, and dancers who do not have an in-depth social dance background and who want to teach beginning social (or ballroom) dance. The material covered in this book is appropriate for any junior high school through adult learner. Specific directions and a variety of approaches will help you better understand the components of effective social dancing, and to teach these components more successfully. It is very satisfying to help students discover the intrinsic rewards possible through social dance: individual skill mastery, an opportunity to meet others, a variety of choices, spontaneous decision making, the joy of moving in unison with a partner to music, and the benefits of a low-impact aerobic workout.

A positive interaction is essential to continued dance participation. The suggestions within this book help you present fun ways of meeting new people, of moving to the music, of practicing good floor and partner etiquette, of effectively leading and following, of executing basics, of adding variations, of combining moves to create routines, and of practicing decision-making situations. Sometimes it is helpful to acknowledge that students may feel frustrated—it happens to everyone who's learning a new skill. As students progress, they can expect that their responses will get easier (with less thinking) and will become more automatic.

This book features a transition from movement terms to dance terms. For example, a gallop is refined to a *triple step* (sometimes called a *shuffle step*) to a *step ball change*—meaning there are three weight changes within two beats of music which are cued by counting "1-and-2."

Another feature is the use of nonsexist terms to indicate both the leader's and the follower's unique roles and responsibilities. Particularly with unequal numbers of males and females, some students may elect to do the opposite role either as a personal challenge, or to dance with a partner. Because the illustrations show a male and a female, the pronouns "his," and "her," have been used to make it easier to follow the illustrations without a lengthy explanation. You'll find it easier to address your comments to the "designated" leader or follower when in a large class. After attempting a different role, students quickly gain an appreciation for their partner, so you might try switching roles for a few minutes, especially early in the learning process when the followers seem to be impatient with the leaders. Because the designated leaders have the most decisions to make, the teaching cues are most often given for them, while the followers do the reverse.

A third feature of this book is the addition of directions and cues for both the American and Latin versions of the cha-cha (the participant's book was limited to the American version). Now, you have the option of teaching either version, keeping in mind that it is easier to stay with one or the other because the teaching cues are different.

A fourth feature of this book is that the learning steps are hierarchically tiered for your ease in individualizing instruction. For a variety of reasons, beginning classes almost always have one or more students who are either novice beginners or more accomplished dancers. Use the suggestions in this book to assess your students' progress starting with their rhythmic competency (ability to walk to an underlying beat) up to their selection of spontaneous sequences most appropriate for a crowded dance floor. Notice that the learning steps within this book are instructor steps (they do *not* correspond with the learner's steps listed in the participant's book).

I've found that once students experience the fun and social side of dance, they are more motivated to learn detailed techniques and characteristic styling points that require their concentration and patience. Share the fun with your students and help get them started on a lifetime of dancing opportunities!

I dedicate this book to my wonderful dance partner and husband, Sam—in loving gratitude for all his patience, support, and encouragement in helping me make my dreams come true.

Implementing the Steps to Success Staircase

This book is meant to be flexible for not only your students' needs but for your needs as well. It is common to hear that students' perceptions of a task change as the task is learned. However, instructors go through learning stages as well (Vickers, 1990).

More experienced or master teachers tend to approach the teaching of activities in a similar manner. They have an in-depth knowledge of the activity, and they plan according to the type of learner as well as to the available equipment and facilities. In addition, they are highly organized (i.e., they do not waste time getting groups together or using long explanations), they briefly explain the importance of skills and concepts within the final performance context, they integrate information (from appropriate subdisciplines), and they quickly place students into realistic practice situations.

The realistic practice situations (called *drills*) within this book prepare students for dancing with a partner on a dance floor with other couples. Each drill is an extension of the previous, slowly building more student responsibility. The drills increase in difficulty by logical manipulations of the following:

- practicing selected parts of a basic step, or portions of a sequence;
- varying direction, level, and range of movement;
- increasing the number of people (e.g., dancing alone, with a partner, with other couples, or with a group);
- changing the conditions of performance, including tempo and rhythm;
- increasing in an accumulative manner the number of partner positions, transitions, and variations used in combination; and
- adding decision-making opportunities and strategies.

Appendix A presents an overview of how the social dance skills and concepts derive from various subdisciplines, such as motor learning, exercise physiology, sport psychology, sport sociology, and other pertinent knowledge bases. You can use this information not only to gain insights into the various interrelationships, but also to define the subject matter for social dance as covered in this instructor's guide.

The following questions offer specific suggestions for implementing this knowledge base within your specific teaching situation(s). Your answers will help you individualize your instruction within a group setting (i.e., a class of 20 to 50 students).

1. Under what conditions do you teach?

   - How much space is available?
   - What is the average class size?
   - How much time is allotted per class session?
   - How many class sessions do you teach?
   - Do you have any teaching assistants?
   - What type of sound system is available?
   - Do you have access to appropriate social dance music?

   This instructor's guide is organized so that you can select any one, two, three, four, or five social dances to present to your students, as appropriate for your situation. Because it is often difficult to find social dance music slow enough for beginners, there are five social dance audiocassettes, each containing 30 minutes of instrumental social dance music, specifically created to accompany the drills in this instructor's guide (see the last page of this book). Also, you may use the soundsheet within the companion, participant's book (*Social Dance: Steps to Success*) for either outside-of-class assignments (see Side A), or as a review (see Side B) of the five dances covered.

2. What are your students' initial skill levels?

   - Who has danced before?
   - What do students want to learn in your class?

- Why are they taking your class (e.g., to meet others, to learn to dance, to fulfill a requirement, or because their partners want them to learn)?

Informal observation is an easy way to identify students' initial skill levels. Expect a range of skill levels from beginner to accomplished. For specific criterion to observe, see the rating charts for each basic dance step (in Step 2) as well as the Keys to Success items within each step. No matter where your students fit, encourage them to pace their practices (and expectations) to fit their own readiness levels instead of comparing themselves with others within the class. Quality of execution (i.e., doing a few things well) is more important then quantity (i.e., doing a lot of things poorly).

3. What is the best order to teach social dance skills?

   - What skills, concepts, and strategies are important to early versus later learning stages?
   - Which dance should you present first?
   - When should you introduce new skills?

Regardless of which dance(s) you select to teach, notice that the instructor steps in this book follow a hierachical arrangement (see Figure 1). Thus, you can work within the various tiers, as appropriate to your situation(s). Step 1 introduces fundamental rhythmic skills and concepts that might be used within a review, or as an orientation experience, or as lead-up experiences within a 3-week rhythmic unit. Step 2 introduces the basic social dance steps, transitions, and partner positions that might be covered within an 8-week social dance or beginning ballroom unit. Steps 3 through 7 build on the basics from Step 2 by adding transitions, partner positions, and step variations that might be included within a 12- or 16-week unit. Then, Step 12 offers fun mixers and challenge situations that may be used at any time within your unit as appropriate to your situation(s).

Use the form in Appendix B.1 to put into order the steps that you will be able to cover in the time available. See Appendix B.2 for suggestions on when to introduce, review, or continue practicing each step.

4. What objectives do you want your students to accomplish by the end of a lesson, unit, or course?

   - How important are social outcomes?
   - How important are performance outcomes?
   - Will both technique and performance objectives be included?

For general objectives, select from the student outcomes listed at the beginning of each step in this book. For technique or qualitative objectives, select from the Student Keys to Success execution techniques listed within each step. For performance or quantitative objectives, select from the Success Goals that are provided with each drill. For cognitive objectives, see the Test Bank for selected written questions.

5. How will you assess your students' progress?

   - What are your grading and evaluation philosophies?
   - How often should students receive input on their progress?

See the Assessing Your Students' Progress section for ideas, suggestions, and sample master forms.

6. Which activities should be selected to achieve student objectives?

   - Which activities will you select?
   - How will you structure each class or lesson?
   - How much will you cover in each class?

Avoid a random approach to selecting drills. Plan enough activities to keep students actively moving and involved versus waiting in line or listening to long explanations. You may modify the blank lesson plan form in Appendix C.1 to best fit your needs. Appendix C.2 shows a sample lesson plan for introducing the triple-lindy swing.

The 83 drills in this book help you to individualize instruction for the "nov-

I. Step 1

Rhythmic experiences to help learners

- identify the beat,
- walk to the beat,
- modify everyday locomotor movements to create rhythmic patterns, and
- combine rhythmic patterns to form simple line and partner dances.

II. Step 2

Practice drills to help learners

- execute the basics within five different dance styles (swing, cha-cha, polka, fox-trot, and waltz),
- add direction changes,
- demonstrate proper partner and floor etiquette,
- transition from one partner position to another position, and
- combine up to three consecutive moves or leads.

III. Steps 3-7

Practice drills and variations to help learners

- execute at least two variations within each partner position,
- add partner positions,
- continue to demonstrate proper partner and floor etiquette,
- combine four or more consecutive moves or leads, and
- make spontaneous decisions on the floor, depending upon the flow of traffic encountered.

IV. Step 8

Practice drills to help learners

- adjust for different tempos and styles of music,
- adjust to different partners,
- switch partners within the same dance,
- create demonstration routines or new variations, and
- problem solve potential dance situations.

Figure 1   Four-tier hierarchical structure outlining the instructor steps in this book.

ice" beginner dancer, the "average" beginner, and the accomplished dance student (see the To Increase Difficulty and To Decrease Difficulty suggestions that extend the basic drill instructions). The drills are specifically designed to help you effectively manage large groups of students. See the key for interpreting the diagrams used in this book.

7. What rules and expectations do you have for your class?

- What are your policies on grades, attendance, absences, and exams?
- What time will your class start and end?

- What attire is appropriate? For example, can students wear tennis shoes, or are leather soles more appropriate for your facility? Can students wear cutoffs with holes in them, or bare-midriff tops in class? Do you expect different attire for different sponsored events (e.g., a Friday night practice versus a monthly dance)?

Read the general class management suggestions and legal duties presented within the Preparing Your Class for Success section. Let your students know what your rules are during your orientation on the first day of class. Consider posting your rules and reviewing them as needed.

Teaching is a complex task, requiring you to make many decisions that affect both you and your students (see Figure 2). Use this book to create an effective and successful learning experience for you and everyone you teach. It is very rewarding to see students smiling and having fun while dancing. Enjoy!

Key

CW = Clockwise

CCW = Counterclockwise

I = Instructor

LOD = Line of direction

L = Left

R = Right

O = Follower

O.F. = Original front

X = Leader

⟶ = Direction of movement

= Follower's footwork (right foot shaded)

= Leader's footwork (right foot shaded)

= Foot prepares to move

= Weight on ball of foot

= No weight on ball of foot

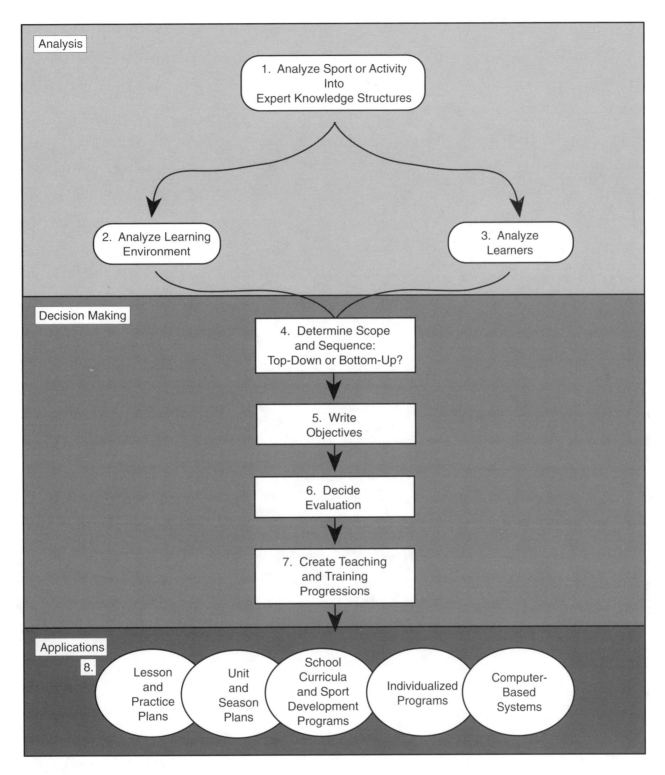

Figure 2   Instructional design model utilizing expert knowledge structures.

Note. From *Instructional Design for Teaching Physical Activities* by J.N. Vickers, 1990, Champaign, IL: Human Kinetics. Copyright by Joan N. Vickers. Reprinted by permission. This instructional design model has appeared in earlier forms in *Badminton: A Structures of Knowledge Approach* (p. 1) by J.N. Vickers and D. Brecht, 1987, Calgary, AB: University Printing Services. Copyright 1987 by Joan N. Vickers; and "The Role of Expert Knowledge Structures in an Instructional Design Model for Physical Education" by J.N. Vickers, 1983, *Journal of Teaching in Physical Education*, **2**(3), p. 20. Copyright 1983 by Joan N. Vickers.

Preparing Your Class for Success

Successful teachers create an effective learning environment, one that is enjoyable, informative, and stimulating to students. Let them know that it is okay to make mistakes—this is the way we learn. This section addresses the following topics: introduction and orientation, class organization, etiquette and attire, learning styles and cue selection, equipment, and legal duties.

INTRODUCTION AND ORIENTATION

Make your students' first impression of your class a positive one so that they will want to continue with social dance classes. During your first class meeting, warmly greet students and welcome them. Instead of taking role by calling their names, you might ask them to introduce themselves, including where they are from and perhaps why they are taking this class, or what they most want to get out of this class. Their answers help you to know how to pronounce students' names as well as gain insights about their particular motivations and expectations. Then, you can provide an overview of the course content (with student choices?), including your rules and expectations on attendance and absences, acceptable attire, and grading. This is also the ideal time to start mixing students socially through fun mixers that permit you to informally observe your students' skill levels.

CLASS ORGANIZATION

Thorough preparation is the key to successful teaching. Planning saves valuable practice time during class and makes the class flow more smoothly. Structure the lesson for as much time-on-task as possible. Include specific formations to keep students moving from one portion of the lesson to the next. Avoid long lines or waiting of any kind. Avoid isolating students by having them dance in front of the rest of the class, unless students choose to do so. Provide time for students to practice and receive your feedback. End the class with a fun activity so that students will be eager to return for more. Thus, this section provides suggestions on how to structure a lesson, on formations to use for quick transitions, and on ways to select partners.

How to Structure a Lesson

The structure of your lesson should gradually increase in intensity and then decrease in intensity as the class ends. This also includes gradually increasing the time that your students are continuously dancing. At the early stages, just getting to the end of one song can be an accomplishment for some students. Later, it is considered good manners to dance with a variety of partners, which also increases the time they dance continuously and strengthens endurance through low-impact cardiovascular exercise.

A sample lesson structure might include the following parts:

a. **Introduction**—Give a brief overview and/or review.
b. **Demonstration**—Present new basic steps, or variations, or combinations, or strategies.
c. **Rehearsal**—Provide students with practice time and feedback.
d. **Culminating Activity**—Ask students to transfer their skills to new situations, such as using the same basic steps within a mixer or experimenting with spontaneous, decision-making situations.
e. **Closure**—Review topics covered, reiterate important points, and bridge to next class.

Provide goals and feedback for each segment of the class as well as for both the leader's and the follower's part. Because there is often only one teacher, it is important to keep all students on task. Avoid letting one part of the class sit or remain unfocused while you work with the other part. Rather, give each a brief overview, and let one group practice while you continue with the other group.

You might consider using videotaped demonstrations if you have access to monitors, VCR equipment, and a partner (or a model couple). The students can learn from observing both partners' parts in unison as well as in isolation. Remember that students will need your input on what to "see" in their performance. At first, they tend to see only aspects about their body type (i.e., too heavy, too thin, too short, too tall, and so forth) until you can refocus their attention to their movements (e.g., footwork placement, direction moved, distance from partner, and so forth).

Use objective, positive feedback whenever possible. Pinpoint the result, and identify how the student can get there. For example, "Rotate your shoulders and upper torso as if you are turning a car wheel 45 degrees to your left" provides more specific information for students to self-correct at a later date. Avoid a negative or vague statement, such as "You did not lead properly."

Formations to Use for Quick Transitions

Select ahead of time which formation will keep students moving from one portion of the lesson to the next. Within each formation, you need to be in a position to command the students' attention at all times. Take into consideration the partner position as well as the amount of space available. The following selected formations are categorized according to their purpose on the dance floor: to remain stationary, or to travel in the LOD.

Stationary Formations

Use the following formations for dances done in one spot (roughly a 5- to 10-ft diameter circle), such as used in the swing or the cha-cha, or for early instruction with any basic step when students start in a stationary position.

Split the Room: Stand in the center with your back to the music. Ask the leaders to stand on your right and the followers to stand on your left. This formation can be either an informal, scattered formation or formal, aligned rows. The advantage of this formation is that students practice in relationship to a partner without having to actually touch a partner. With very large classes, you will need to periodically rotate the back row to the front row and have all other rows move back, so that you can see them and they can see you.

Continuous "S" Rotation: With your back to the music, face the rows of partners. Ask only the followers (or only the leaders) in the first line to move clockwise to the next partner. The last designated mover in the first row goes to the next row, and the designated persons move counterclockwise to the next partner. The last designated mover in the second row goes to the third row, and the designated persons move clockwise to the next partner, and so forth (see Figure 3). With very large classes, allow enough time for the last designated mover (who has the farthest distance to travel) to pair up with the next partner in the first row.

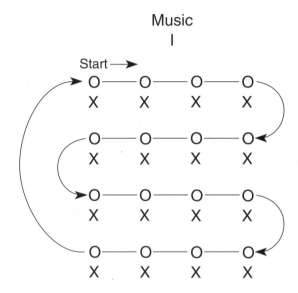

Figure 3   Continuous "S" rotation.

Transition to Partner Rows: From the split-the-room formation, have the leaders and followers turn toward the center of the room to face each other. Ask the leaders to walk forward, passing right shoulders until the first leader in each row meets the last follower in that row (see Figure 4a), and all are paired up. Then, adjust the space in-between to be more equidistant (see Figure 4b). If there are extra persons, then space them such that no two persons without a partner are next to each other. In early learning stages, it is helpful to have all students facing the same front.

LOD Formations

Use the following formations either after your students are comfortable traveling the length (or width) of the room, or whenever you want

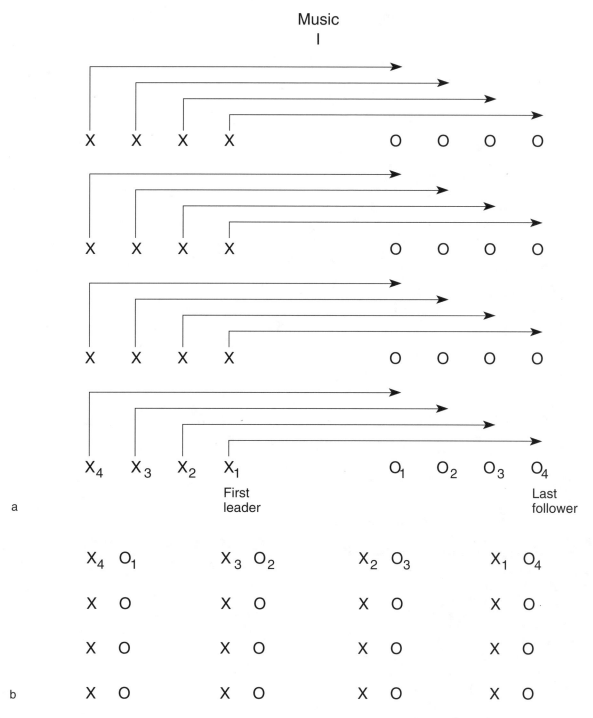

Figure 4 Transition from a split-the-room formation to partner rows: (a) first leader moves to the last follower in line, then (b) the couples space out.

to keep students moving continuously in the Line-of-Direction (LOD). The LOD is the counterclockwise traveling direction around the perimeter of the room that is used within the fox-trot, waltz, and polka.

Single Circle: Without partners, ask the stu-

dents to make a single circle facing counterclockwise. This formation is useful when students need to practice without a partner and travel in the LOD.

Double Circle: To move from a single to a double circle, alternately designate one person to be on the outside circle, and the next person to be in the inner circle. Each circle may face a different direction, e.g., if you want the leaders to do their part while facing LOD, and the followers to do their part while facing reverse LOD. Or, if you want to pair up partners, designate the first couple, ask them to stand beside each other with their left shoulder toward the center of the circle and face LOD. Continue around the circle until pairs are formed (see Figure 5).

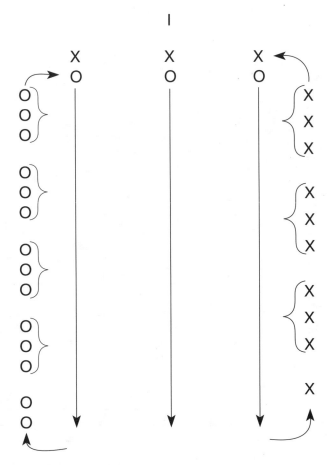

Figure 6 Rotation formation from two lines to waves.

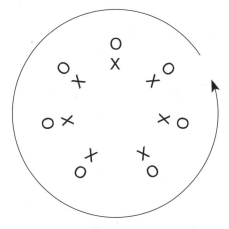

Figure 5 Double-circle formation with leaders on the inside.

If you do not have equal numbers, either ask for volunteers to role play a different part, or, space extras in-between any two pairs of dancers (avoid placing two or more extra persons together). Then, rotate students so that every dancer gets a partner more often.

Lines to Waves: Stand in the center, facing the length of the room. Ask the followers to line up on your right side and the leaders to line up on your left side. As an example, direct three from each side to come toward you, spread out, align with a partner, and travel down the length of the room. After the first row of pairings travel approximately a quarter the length of the room, the next wave of pairings can begin. At the end of the room, they separate and circle back to their respective sides, ready to pair up with new partners (see Figure 6). As space permits, you may align six or more couples in order to more quickly change partners and minimize waiting.

Ways to Select Partners

When in a social setting, students want to meet others, so it is helpful to frequently rotate partners. Use humor as you explain the rationale for changing partners to avoid any potential accusations and to permit more practice time on leading and following (for example, let them know that they are not marrying this partner!). Avoid letting students select the same partner or be inconsiderate, in any way, of other classmembers. One of the goals in social dancing is to be comfortable dancing with others. Thus, during early learning stages, consider matching students in creative ways. You may use any of the previous formation examples or select from some of the following options for matching partners:

- Ask students to match up with someone that they have not yet danced with.

- Ask students to go to the perimeter of the room, and designate either the leaders or the followers to rotate to the next person closest to them.
- Give students two or three task options, and let them match partners according to their preference (e.g., to practice alone, or with a partner using a set sequence, or with a partner using spontaneous sequences).
- Be creative with name tags, clothing colors, locations in the room, or other ways to match students, such as drawing a number (prepare two sets of numbers, one for leaders and one for followers to select from) as they arrive to class; let them find the person with the same number.

If you happen to have a few couples in class who want to stay together, you may want to compromise with them by rotating only during a portion of the class and giving them some practice time together (however, remind them that they will eventually be better leaders and followers if they have practiced with others [rotating gives students more trial-and-error practice and tends to eliminate arguments]). If the entire class is matched up with partners who do not want to switch, then consider letting them stay with their chosen partners, and occasionally mix partners during mixers. As students gain more self-confidence, they will be more willing to dance with different partners.

ETIQUETTE AND ATTIRE

There are two types of etiquette that are integrated throughout this book: partner and floor. Attire will affect both types of etiquette.

Partner Etiquette

Because the learning process can be frustrating, be aware of instances when students may be inappropriately taking their frustration out on their partners. It is okay to be frustrated. Ask students who are having difficulties to check with you, as an outside observer, to identify and correct the problem. Be aware that a student's body language may also be interpreted as critical feedback (for example, when a student makes a face or is not willing

to dance with a particular partner). Remind students that one of the social benefits of dancing is the opportunity to meet others. Thus, students need to dance with a variety of partners and treat each partner with respect. This is especially important if you are working with students who are hesitant to touch others, or who may have a body odor, or who are unfamiliar with most of the other classmembers. Ask the class to tell you (not their partner) if there is a problem. Avoid stating a particular name, and do not tell the person directly. Instead, make a general announcement to the entire class (e.g., that they need to be more conscious of personal grooming and bathing, or to feel free to request individual feedback, and so forth).

Other general rules for partner etiquette include the following:

- Be responsible for your own actions.
- Do not give advice unless asked for (this includes criticism).
- Trust that your partner will do the correct action as soon as he or she can possibly do so.
- State a request starting with "Would you please . . . [state action in positive way!]."
- Ask your instructor for clarification.
- Thank your partner.
- Introduce yourself to a new partner.

Floor Etiquette

The type of dance determines where students locate themselves on the dance floor. There is an outer, fast lane for dances that travel in the LOD. The next inner lane is for dances that start and stop. The center of the floor is for spot dances that are executed within a small area. Figure 7 shows these floor locations. Students should avoid bumping into other couples on the dance floor. If a collision does occur, ask students to apologize or excuse themselves. Remind students that they need to look over the right shoulder of their partner in order to survey the floor traffic and adjust their movements accordingly.

Attire

Typically, the proper attire for social dance should reflect the situation, ranging from informal to formal. For safety reasons, stress

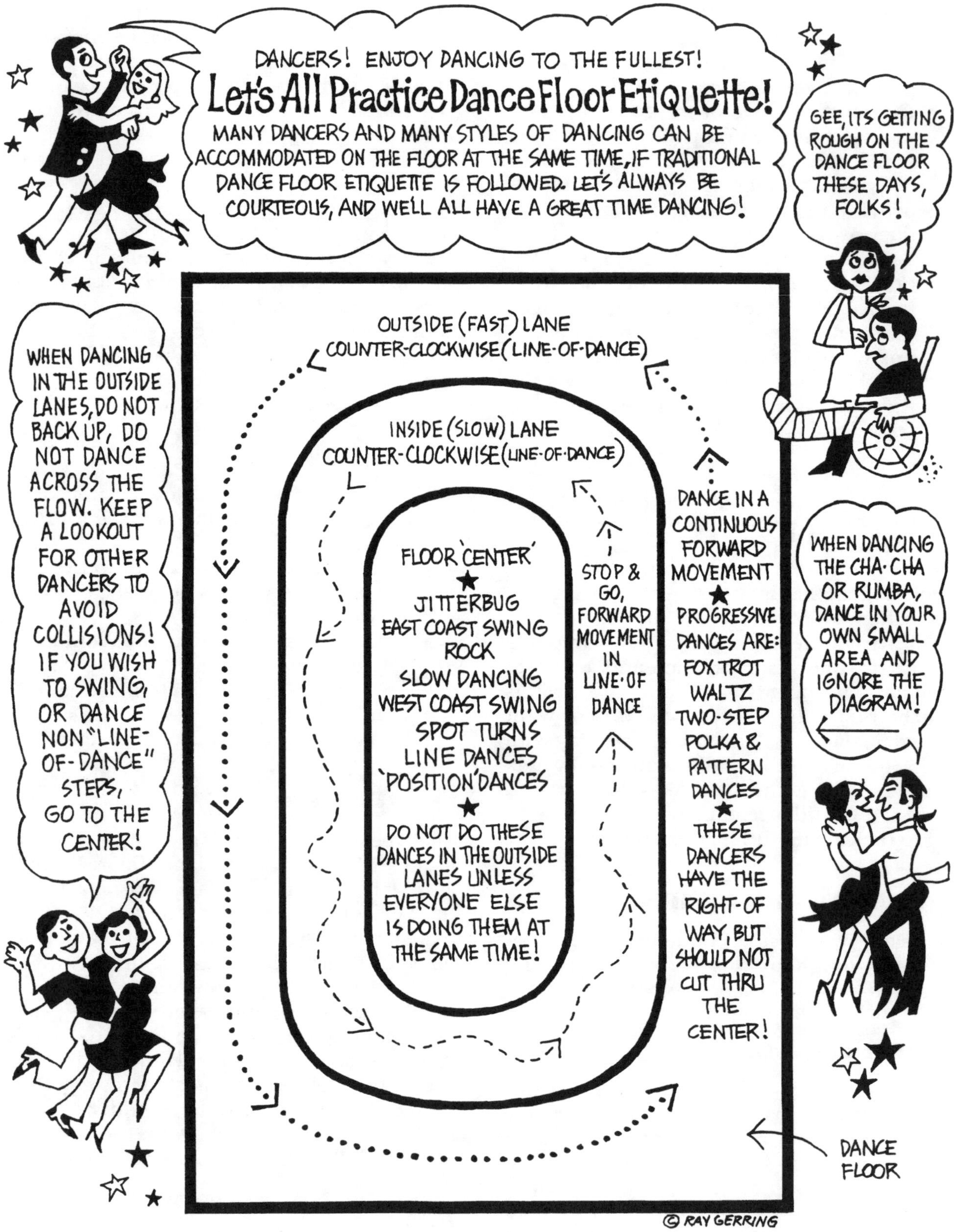

Figure 7   Good floor etiquette is a must.

the appropriate shoe sole for the floor available. On some floors, the same shoes that were worn outside would damage the floor, while other floors are so slippery that rubber soles are needed for traction. Generally, a leather-sole or a special, felt-like dance sole facilitates execution during turns; stocking feet are too slippery (and can be painful, if the toes are stepped on). In addition, explain and recommend the "proper" attire for ballroom dance situations: either a skirt and blouse or dress for women and good slacks and a clean shirt for men or more formal evening wear, depending upon the situation. Because a more formal attire will yield more formal manners, students may not consider the importance of etiquette when they are in less formal attire. For this reason, you should stress etiquette regardless of attire. Avoid requiring a specific attire and basing grades on the attire actually worn (see Legal Duty #7 on page 9).

LEARNING STYLES AND CUE SELECTION

Because there are different learning styles, it is important to use a variety of cues. However, to avoid confusing students in the early stages of learning, use only one presentation method at a time (Weikart, 1989). For example, demonstrate without talking (for visual learners), or talk without moving your hands and body (for auditory learners), or, position students' hands, feet, and arms (for kinesthetic learners). In addition, some learners may need to vocalize the counts (or, have one partner call the selected cues for the couple). Eventually, they will be able to mentally repeat the appropriate cue.

Select the appropriate verbal cue(s) for your learners. Sample types of cues follow.

- tempo (i.e., slow, moderate, or fast)
- direction (i.e., forward, backward, left, right, diagonal, or turning)
- specific foot (i.e., left, or right)
- counts (e.g., rhythmic pattern "a, 1-and-2")
- underlying beats (i.e., whole counts grouped in either three or four counts)
- rhythm (i.e., slow or quick)
- weight transfer or nonweight transfer (e.g., "step, ball, change" refers to weight changes, while "touch," "kick," and so forth, refers to actions without a weight change)

Foot Position Cues

Balance and styling is improved when students place their feet properly. The basic foot positions transfer from ballet and may be modified slightly (for example, when feet are in a parallel position instead of a turned-out position). The most common foot positions used in social dance are first, second, third, fourth, and fifth (see Figure 8). You may choose to not use the ballet terms and just describe the specific foot positions as they are used within the various basic steps. The more accomplished students become, the more they should have their feet in a specific position (whether or not they know each foot position by name).

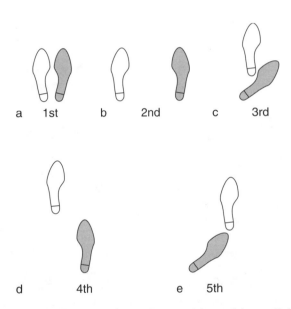

Figure 8 Common dance foot positions: (a) parallel first, (b) parallel second, (c) third, (d) parallel fourth, and (e) fifth.

Integrating Footwork With the Music

The selected cues used in this book highlight the relationship between both spatial and temporal aspects of performance. Do not cue the footwork actions in isolation of the music (without intent). That is, do not say "1, 2, 3" to indicate three footwork actions within two beats of music. Rather, use the verbal cues "1-and-2" to distinguish that there are three footwork actions within two beats of music, blending the footwork with the timing execution.

Also, it is helpful to give students both tempo and starting cues. For example, you might mentally count to yourself on "1, 2, 3, 4" (or "1, 2, 3"), then give verbal cues "5, 6, 7, 8" (or "4, 5, 6"). The first count of a measure is called the *downbeat*, which you can help students recognize when you say it with more force than the other counts.

EQUIPMENT

Depending upon your present equipment, budget, and class size, you will need

- a reliable sound system, such as a stereo turntable and appropriate records, an audiocassette player and appropriate audiocassettes,* or a CD player and appropriate CDs;
- a remote control for music, if possible; and
- some type of microphone (wireless is ideal), which helps save your voice if you teach multiple classes.

No matter what type of audio equipment you prefer or have available, there is no substitute for planning. Hunting for a particular tempo or song during class wastes class time. Also, students like to hear a variety of songs. Consider preparing a master list of the songs' locations, or pre-cue, or pre-record your music selections in the desired order. If students want to bring in their own music, ask them to do so well in advance so that you'll have an opportunity to preview the selections to determine how you might (or might not) use them during class.

Optional equipment includes a videotape camera, a tripod, a monitor, name tags, a bulletin board, a small cassette recorder and audiocassettes* for students to check out practice music (with some limitations, e.g., while in the building or for only a short time), and videotapes or films of dancers in action (as models of what to expect or what will be covered).

LEGAL DUTIES

As a teacher, you have certain legal responsibilities to your students. Failure to fulfill these duties may constitute negligence on your part and have serious legal consequences (Nygaard & Boone, 1985). The following eight duties are appropriate for consideration when teaching a social dance class:

1. Adequate Supervision

   Position yourself so that you are in command of your entire class. Make frequent visual scans to check for any students not on task, and refocus them, as appropriate, to the task. Do not permit any behavior that may be hazardous to others. Never leave your class unsupervised, turn your back, or allow students to leave, except in an emergency.

2. Sound Planning

   Select drills and formations appropriate for the age and ability of your students. Present drills in an appropriate progression from basic to complex, and center them around a theme or objective. Organize both your instructions and your transitions between drills to avoid creating situations where students are congested or during which students are waiting around.

3. Inherent Risks

   Advise students that certain inherent risks accompany participation in any physical activity. In social dance, students can minimize risks by using correct skill execution, maintaining physical fitness, practicing in a controlled manner by not bumping into others, and not wearing dangling jewelry that could interfere with their dancing.

4. Safe Learning Environment

   A safe environment includes an open, unobstructed dance area and an uncluttered area surrounding the dance floor, as well as enough space to allow a safe distance among the couples. Consider the following suggestions:

   - Clarify and enforce the floor etiquette rules regarding the flow of traffic.
   - Review the building's assigned escape route in case of fire or other emergency. You should point out the

---

*See the last page of this book for information on five, 30-minute audiocassettes of instrumental music specifically prepared with slow-to-fast tempos for five social dances: swing, cha-cha, fox-trot, waltz, and polka.

exits to your class during a safety orientation.

- Check for proper illumination and ventilation.
- Keep the dance area free of obstacles (such as chairs, tables, stray paper, or puddles of water). Dancers need an uncluttered, open area.
- Have a plan for controlling the flow of spectators and visitors during class. In a few instances, it may be advantageous to allow students from another class to join in, especially if there are uneven numbers. However, consider restricting spectators and non-enrolled students because they put more pressure on students, especially in the early learning stages, and because you are liable for any injuries sustained by non-enrolled students.
- Have students keep valuables in lockers or other safe places to avoid potential thefts (this likelihood is increased whenever spectators are permitted).

5. Evaluating Students' Physical Status for Activity

You should make each student's existing physical conditions part of your records, noting any condition that may cause pain, injury, or impede movement during class so that you may make appropriate allowances for the individual's disability and devise ways that they will be successful.

6. Emergency First Aid Procedures

In the event of an accident, you must be prepared to provide adequate medical assistance. It is your duty to your students to have planned, posted medical procedures that can be put into immediate action. This includes knowing how to immediately summon the aid of an available doctor, nurse, or paramedic; have their phone numbers with you at all times.

7. Specific Legal Concerns

You cannot restrict your classes or your students in a way that violates their civil rights. In social dance, you must be careful about placing arbitrary restrictions on the appearance, conduct, or free expression of your students. It is difficult for you to control your students' dress code or the way they wear their hair unless safety is a factor (e.g., shoes with rubber soles may grip too much and cause an injury). Avoid discrimination, especially on the basis of race, sex, or handicapping conditions. You also have a legal duty to protect the civil rights of any spectators, if permitted.

8. General Legal Concerns

You definitely need to be aware of the possibilities for liability (e.g., risks when transporting students, especially when using personal vehicles) and must take adequate measures to protect yourself. Always keep accurate records of your activities, especially in the event of an accident involving an injury. Keep such records for a minimum of 5 years. It is wise for all instructors to carry adequate personal liability insurance.

Step 1   Checking Students' Rhythmic Skills

Students' confidence levels increase when they understand how to create a rhythmic pattern, how to match their footwork to the beats of the music, how to be in balance, and how to put together parts to form a dance. In social dancing situations, students are dancing whenever they are repeating rhythmic patterns. A rhythmic pattern is a series of weight changes or actions with a recurring series of beats. Ranging from easy to difficult, rhythmic patterns blend footwork with various musical selections. Some musical selections may have a consistent beat and tempo, while others may include complex factors, such as syncopation and dynamics, that make it more difficult for students to "find" the beat. Early in learning, it is not necessary to use musical accompaniment; rather, ask students to match footwork to the counts that you cue for them, thereby giving you more control over the tempo. When you observe that students are ready, introduce slow music that has a distinguishable beat, and gradually increase the tempo.

By the end of this instructor step, your students should be able to

- walk to a beat (adjusting to either counts or music),
- repeat a rhythmic pattern for the length of one song, and
- demonstrate both even and uneven rhythmic patterns.

THREE FUNDAMENTAL SKILLS

Three critical skills provide the foundation for rhythmic patterns (see Figure 1.1). These skills are hierarchically arranged, as follows:

1. Hearing the beat and rhythm (perceptual skill)
2. Executing movements with balance and control (motor skill)
3. Coinciding footwork with the music (perceptual-motor match)

You can facilitate the learning process by helping students connect their footwork with the music, which integrates the perceptual and motor aspects of their performance (making a perceptual-motor match). If you notice that certain students have difficulty walking to a steady beat (or count), then observe each of the fundamental skills to identify where the problem lies (see Figure 1.1). As appropriate, you may refer these students to specific drills within Steps 1-3 of their partici-

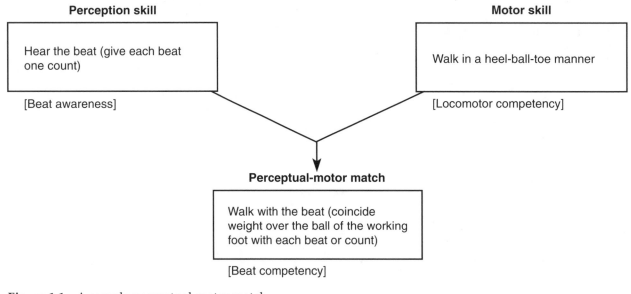

Figure 1.1   A sample perceptual-motor match.

pant's book either for outside-of-class assignments or individual review (before or after class), and you can use the suggestions for decreasing the difficulty level that are included with each drill (later in this chapter).

The easiest way to find out whether students can integrate perceptual and motor skills is to ask them to walk to a beat (using either counts or music). This task (which demonstrates *beat competency*) can be fun when presented in the form of line dances, partner-patterned dances, and mixers that do not yet require leading and following responsibili-

ties. Students display a variety of skill levels; some progress faster than others. Informally observe your students' execution of at least one of the following three selected locomotor movements with musical accompaniment. These movements are used in the drills at the end of this step. If you have limited time, use only Drill 7. With practice, you can quickly develop a trained eye for differentiating a range of skill levels from beginning to accomplished. The following perceptual-motor match rating chart provides sample observation criteria.

Perceptual-Motor Match Rating Chart

BEAT COMPETENCY	BEGINNING	ACCOMPLISHED
Walks	• Walks forward using a sliding motion on ball of feet • Walks with various parts of the foot hitting the floor with each beat or count	• Walks forward using a heel-ball-toe motion • Coordinates walks by coinciding the body's weight over the ball of the working foot with each beat or count
Hops	• Little to no knee bend to push off and land • Inconsistent landing with counts	• Same knee bends to both push off and absorb landing force • Coordinates hops to coincide the landing either on a whole count (even rhythm) or a partial count (uneven rhythm)
Triple Steps	• Lets feet pass on the "and" count • Takes three regular walking steps in three counts (1, 2, 3); no observable "right or left side" (treats triple steps like three-beat even rhythms—giving each step one count)	• Keeps the "and" foot trailing (behind) the lead foot • Groups three weight changes (step, ball, step, or step, ball, change) in two counts (1-and-2) on each side (understands the uneven rhythm concept—giving the second step half a count)

You may also combine these movements, for example, a step and a hop, or a schottische (three walks and a hop).

RHYTHMIC CONCEPTS: STUDENT KEYS TO SUCCESS

Depending upon your students' experience, you may use the drills in this instructor step at least three ways: (a) as a mini-unit devoted to line and partner dances in order to teach the prerequisite skills and concepts that students need to progress, (b) as a one-day orientation or an introduction to a unit by using only Drill 7 (circle mixer), and (c) as a way to informally observe students' entry skills. Select those drills most appropriate for your situation. The drills in this step provide fun ways to introduce and help students understand the following concepts:

1. *How to coincide the body's weight over the ball of the working foot with each beat of the music.* Various parts of the foot may hit the floor during a walking step. Some students are neither aware of the potential variety nor which part of the foot should coincide with each count or beat of the music (see Figure 1.2).

2. *The faster the tempo, the shorter the step length.* A slow tempo has the advantage of giving students more time to react. Many actions are required within a very short period of time. For example, when walking forward, the heel contacts the floor, then the ball of foot contacts the floor and the body's weight transfers over the ball of the foot—all coinciding with Count 1; then, the toe pushes off as the next step is taken.

3. *Group walking steps in fours or threes in order to have a definite starting and ending place.* Students may not know when to start with the music because the beats seem to run continuously. Showing the connection between footwork and the beats per measure helps students see the structure of music. The first beat of the measure is called the downbeat, and the second beat is the upbeat. In 4/4 time, four beats occur within one measure. In 3/4 time, three beats occur within one measure. In 2/4 time, two beats occur within one measure (see Figure 1.3). Sometimes it is easier to group two measures of 2/4 time together and count four beats, especially when students

Figure 1.2 Weight transfers forward from (a) a heel strike to (b) over ball of working foot on each beat.

are executing two triple steps—one triple step on each side of the body (e.g., stepping right, left, right, then left, right, left). Grouping two measures gives students an early awareness of phrasing, and it gives you more time to verbally cue students with a faster tempo.

4. *There are two types of rhythmic patterns: even and uneven.* In even rhythmic patterns, there is either a weight change or an action getting one count, for example, walk, run, hop, schottische, or waltz. Uneven rhythmic patterns combine whole and partial counts, for example, when the triple-step verbal cue counts are "1-and-2," tell students that there are three weight changes or actions within two beats of music. The triple step, used in swing, cha-cha, and polka, and the hop, used in polka, are uneven rhythmic pattern examples. Another example of an uneven rhythmic pattern is taking only one step within two beats of music, which occurs later in the magic step (fox-trot) and in the single lindy (swing).

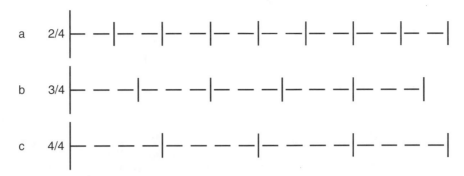

Figure 1.3   Underlying beats per measure for (a) 2/4 time, (b) 3/4 time, and (c) 4/4 time.

5. *Repeat a rhythmic pattern at least twice before changing or modifying it.* This gives students more time to react to the rhythmic pattern before having to do another one, which is helpful in early learning stages.

6. *Start with short routines that have two parts, A and B, then alternate ABAB for the length of a song.* This permits students to be aware of how to choreograph a simple routine and lets them have some fun because they are dancing within a very short time.

7. *Within a routine, mixing even and uneven rhythmic patterns is more difficult than using either all even or all uneven rhythmic patterns.* Gradually introduce students to more difficult patterns. Start with even rhythmic patterns, then move to uneven rhythmic patterns, and lastly mix rhythmic patterns within the AB parts of a routine. Be ready to either modify the parts or to practice the parts separately, if students are having difficulties.

Detecting and Correcting Rhythmic Pattern Errors

Students often need feedback on three types of problems: knowing when to move with the music (beat awareness), maintaining balance and proper alignment while moving, and connecting their footwork with the music

(beat competency). It will be easier for you to help students with difficulties in execution and timing. Postural deviations require a great deal of student discipline and desire to change.

ERROR

CORRECTION

Beat Awareness

1. Difficulty in recognizing the beat of the music.

1. Point out that the words, melody and song rhythm are unreliable cues to follow. A more consistent musical cue is the underlying beat, which is typically played by the drums or brass instruments (heavier sounds). Pretape song segments for extra practice (as part of your class review).

ERROR   **CORRECTION**

2. Inconsistent starts or not knowing when to start with the music.

2. Have the students narrow their focus (perhaps closing their eyes) in order to block out all other distractions in the room and listen for the beat, which gives them the tempo. Encourage them to count in groups of either threes or fours (either verbally or mentally). The students must be ready to start walking at the established tempo (giving each beat one count). Ask them to lift the heel of their working foot slightly off the floor in order to more quickly overcome inertia and be ready to step onto that foot on the downbeat.

Alignment and Balance

1. The student's pelvic girdle is not centered.

1. Students need a kinesthetic awareness of body position. Suspend, or have the students visualize, a plumb line from the ceiling. Ask students to stand with either shoulder along the side of the plumb line. The plumb line should cross the following body parts: ear, shoulder, hip, knee, and ankle. Another option is to videotape or photograph the students' standing alignment. Check whether the students have sufficient lower back flexibility and abdominal strength. If not, refer the students to appropriate fitness texts for directions on how to do exercises such as a pelvic tilt and curl-ups.

2. Students watch either their own or their partner's feet.

2. Encourage students to look at an object that is level with their eye height (e.g., pick out a crack or line on the wall or look in the LOD or the reverse LOD). Also, ask students to mentally picture what their feet are doing and to use their peripheral vision. Once students do not have to think about their footwork, this error is less commonly encountered.

ERROR 🚫

CORRECTION

3. The students' body weight is back over their heels, and their footwork timing is late when coordinated with music or counts.

3. Ask students to stand with their back against a wall and to notice which part of their body moves away first when they try to take a walking step forward. They will discover that the upper body moves away first, which transfers their body weight forward over the balls of their feet (into a ready position commonly used in most sports). This position can also be achieved by asking students to raise their heels approximately 1/8 inch off the floor, which shifts the body weight over the balls of their feet and permits them to be able to tap their heels. This body weight shift will later be a nonverbal signal that the leader wants to move forward (when in closed or two-hands joined dance positions).

4. Students' feet are angled with toes-out when stepping forward.

4. Students need to keep their feet parallel and approximately 2 to 3 inches apart as if they are standing in narrow railroad tracks. Maintaining a small space in-between the feet will later let a partner step (either forward or backward) without stepping on the other partner's feet.

5. Students slide their feet along the floor, keeping the weight on the balls of their feet when stepping forward.

5. Check that students are using a heel-ball-toe motion during a basic forward walk. Then, observe that the reverse occurs during a backward walk (toe-ball-heel).

Beat Competency

1. Students do not match their footwork actions with your verbal cues.

1. Remind students that your verbal cues tell them when to take a step (transfer weight as they hear the count) or to do an action (nonweight transfer) because you call the action by name, such as "kick."

2. Students let their feet pass (one moves ahead of the other) on the "and" count during the triple steps.

2. Because the "and" count gets half a beat, it also gets half a foot action, or only the "ball" of the foot. The verbal cues tell students this when you say "step, ball, step," or "step, ball, change."

Drills for Developing Rhythmic Skills

1. Metronome Challenge

Purpose and Organization

- This ear-foot teaser is especially helpful for students without any previous rhythmic experiences, and as a refresher for more experienced students (some students do not know how they do something).
- Explain the challenge within a small semicircle; ask students to spread out to make a circle, and to face the counterclockwise (CCW) direction.

Equipment

- A metronome set to click at 100 beats per minute (or use a pre-recorded metronome beat).

Instructions to Class

- "You've heard of brain teasers. This is a foot teaser because I'm going to ask you to think about and notice which part of your foot hits the floor when you walk to metronome clicks. You may start with either foot and walk at your own pace." [Start the clicks, then stop after you have had time to observe the students' variations.]
- "Which part of your foot hit the floor? [Answers should include: heel, ball (with weight back, then centered, then forward over the ball of the foot), and toe with a push-off onto the next step forward.] From these possibilities, you need to coincide (exactly match) your weight over the ball of your working foot with the clicks. Now, try it."

Student Options

- "Start walking whenever you are ready."
- "Start with either foot."

Student Keys to Success

- Use a heel-ball-toe motion on forward walks and a toe-ball-heel motion on backward walks.
- Coincide weight over the ball of each working foot (on forward walks) with each whole count of the music.

Student Success Goal

- 45 seconds of forward walking to the metronome clicks.

To Decrease Difficulty

- Set metronome to 80 beats per minute.
- Use slow counts instead of the metronome clicks.
- Ask students to call out their own counts and correspond the counts with their footwork.

To Increase Difficulty

- Set metronome to 120 beats per minute.
- Reverse direction to walk backward. Warn students to look over one shoulder in order to avoid bumping into anyone. [This experience gives the leaders an appreciation for what the followers do most of the time with a partner.]
- Group eight walks in eight counts: walk forward, then backward.
- Alternately group eight walks in eight counts (forward, then backward), then four walks in four counts (forward, then backward).
- Substitute 4/4-time music for the clicks.

2. Even Rhythmic Patterns

Purpose and Organization

- Grouping counts into measures helps students understand when to start and stop their footwork with the music (instead of the continuous metronome clicks that have no definite start or stop). This drill provides both 4/4-time and 3/4-time rhythmic pattern examples that take either a weight change or an action (nonweight change) on each whole count—using an even rhythm.
- This drill introduces the schottische, which combines three walks and a hop (in folk dance) or substitutes a nonweight action, such as a scuff, kick, or heel slap, for the hop (in country western dance).
- Set up students in a scattered formation facing one wall.

Instructions to Class

- "It is very difficult to know when to start with the metronome clicks because there is no obvious starting or stopping point, just continuous clicks. Notice that music, however, is grouped into a certain number of beats, such as four or three."

With Four Beats to a Measure

- "When four beats are grouped together, it is called 4/4 time (i.e., four beats per measure with each quarter note getting one count"—see Figure 1.4). [Provide a sample of 4/4-time music for students to hear.].
- "An even rhythmic pattern occurs whenever you match a footwork action to each whole count of the measure. One even rhythmic pattern commonly found in line dances is a three-count vine (or grapevine) step. Because line dances may start with either foot first, you'll need to become ambidextrous. Start with your left foot for practice. Take a step to the side on Count 1, cross your right foot behind your left on Count 2, and take another step to your left on Count 3. On Count 4, do a nonweight-change action. There are many action options, such as a toe point (to front, side, back, and so forth), a kick, a hitch (i.e., lift knee with lower leg

angled across the other leg and ankle flexed), a heel, and so forth. Do a scuff for now by flexing, swinging your right ankle and your lower leg in an arc that lets your heel brush the floor without changing your weight."
- "Repeat the three-count vine to your right."
- "You may also travel forward and backward while doing a schottische. Starting with your left foot, take three walks forward, then scuff with your right heel. Now starting with your right foot, take three walks backward, and do a scuff with your left heel."

With Three Beats to a Measure

- "When three beats are grouped together, it is called 3/4 time (i.e., three beats per measure with each quarter note getting one count). [Provide a sample of waltz music for students to hear.] Take three steps sideward (L and R), then forward and backward."
- "Starting with your left foot, take a side step to your left on Count 1, bring your right foot beside your left (or close your foot) on Count 2, and step onto your left foot on Count 3. Repeat these three steps to the right side, connecting them to Counts 4, 5, 6. Repeat both sides. Change weight on *each* count."
- "Take your left step forward on Count 1, bring your right foot beside your left on Count 2, then step onto your left foot on Count 3. With your right foot, take a step backward on Count 4, bring your left foot beside your right foot on Count 5, and step onto your right foot on Count 6. Repeat both directions to counts, then to slow music."

Student Options

- "After you feel comfortable, try substituting another nonweight action in the 4/4-time example, such as a heel slap, a kick, or a toe point."
- "Add a travel turn (see Figure 1.5) on the sideward three counts. Your toes should point to the side, back, and front as you make three weight changes."

Student Keys to Success

- Either a weight change or a nonweight action occurs on each whole count.

Student Success Goal

- Repeat until comfortable, using counts, then slow music.

To Decrease Difficulty

- Use only sideward directions, then add forward and backward directions.
- Freeze each foot position, and match it to the appropriate whole count.

To Increase Difficulty

- Start with the opposite (i.e., right) foot.
- Use a variety of music.

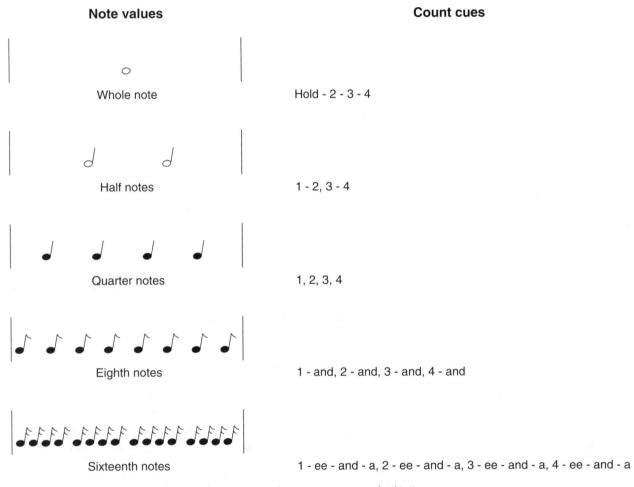

Note values	Count cues
Whole note	Hold - 2 - 3 - 4
Half notes	1 - 2, 3 - 4
Quarter notes	1, 2, 3, 4
Eighth notes	1 - and, 2 - and, 3 - and, 4 - and
Sixteenth notes	1 - ee - and - a, 2 - ee - and - a, 3 - ee - and - a, 4 - ee - and - a

Figure 1.4   Sample note values and count cues for one measure of 4/4 time.

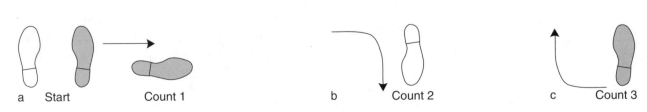

a   Start   Count 1

b   Count 2

c   Count 3

Figure 1.5   A right travel turn is an option during a three-count vine to the right side.

3. Two-Part Sequences

Purpose and Organization

- Simple line dances are sequenced into parts that are repeated for the length of a song. This drill gives an even rhythmic pattern example that is sequenced in two parts, A and B, that are alternately repeated to form an ABAB sequence.
- Set up in a scattered formation, facing one wall.

Instructions to Class

- "A simple line dance is choreographed in two parts, called A and B, that are alternated for the length of a song in an ABAB sequence."

With Four Beats to a Measure

- "Do four schottisches (to L, to R, to L, to R), and call it Part A. Part A takes 16 counts."
- "Add Part B by alternately taking a step, then a scuff. Repeat for a total of eight counts."
- "Now put both parts together."

With Three Beats to a Measure

- "In the previous drill you created an ABAB sequence with three beats to a measure. Review that ABAB sequence. Now, add Part C by traveling forward two basics, and traveling backward two basics. Repeat this three-part sequence (ABCABC) to counts, then to music."

Student Option

- "Add a travel turn on either (or both) side(s)."

Student Keys to Success

- Either change weight or execute a nonweight action (e.g., scuff) on each whole count.

Student Success Goal

- Repeat both sequences for the length of one song.

To Decrease Difficulty

- Practice each part separately using slow counts.
- Use slow music.

To Increase Difficulty

- Use a variety of music styles (such as country, popular, folk, disco, or rock).
- Modify the two-part sequence to become a two-wall dance (see Drill 5) by asking students to slowly rotate to turn 180 degrees during Part B. One solution is to turn a bit on each step, and scuff in place. Thus, it takes two step-scuffs to make a quarter turn, then two more step-scuffs to face the back. Repeat the sequence while facing this new direction.
- Add either a half or a full turn somewhere in the three-part sequence.

4. Uneven Rhythmic Patterns

Purpose and Organization

- This drill provides one example of an uneven rhythmic pattern by adding an "and" count within each two beats or counts (called triple steps, or step-ball-change, or shuffle steps).
- Set up in a scattered formation facing one wall.

Instructions to Class

- "With this example of an uneven rhythmic pattern you'll need to squeeze three weight changes within two counts or beats. The verbal cues are '1-and-2.' Take

a step forward on Count 1. On 'and,' place the ball of your trailing foot slightly behind the heel of your lead (front) foot, and transfer your weight onto it. This results in a pushing action. Take another step forward on Count 2. Repeat these triple steps on both sides of your body."
- "Now try the triple steps backward. Take a backward step on Count 1. On 'and,' place the ball of your trailing foot slightly in front of your lead foot's big toe (do not pass your heels). Then take another backward step on Count 2. Repeat on both sides."

- "Create a two-part sequence by repeating four triple steps forward, then four triple steps backward."

Student Options

- "Do the triple steps at your own tempo."
- "Vary your starting foot."

Student Keys to Success

- The same foot leads on each whole count cued.
- Repeat on both sides of the body.
- There is a weight change on each count cued, i.e., three weight changes.
- On each whole count, use a heel-ball-toe action traveling forward and a toe-ball-heel action traveling backward.
- Use only the ball of your foot on the "and."

Student Success Goal

- Repeat this two-part sequence for the length of one slow song (4/4 time).

To Decrease Difficulty

- Practice only the push-step executed with the ball of the foot, then a walking step (Counts "and-2").
- Do the triple step only in one direction.
- Use slow counts, matching weight changes.

To Increase Difficulty

- Practice starting with either foot.
- Do two triple steps forward, then two triple steps backward.
- Alternately do four triple steps forward and four triple steps backward, then two triple steps forward and two triple steps backward. This is an example of decelerated rhythm.
- Do four triple steps forward, rock your weight forward, backward, forward, backward, do four triple steps backward, and rock your weight backward, forward, backward, forward. Keep the feet in a forward-backward stride position during the rocks (do not move feet; rather, shift weight).
- Add a half turn in-between any of the triple steps.

5. *Intermixing Rhythmic Patterns*

Purpose and Organization

- Students learn how to use their midline as part of their orientation when facing different walls of the room (i.e., they have a left and a right side, according to where their own midline is facing).
- This drill intermixes uneven and even rhythmic patterns and introduces a pivot turn.
- Set up facing one wall.

Instructions to Class

- "If a dance starts over while you're facing either the front or the back wall, it is called a two-wall line dance. Try the following parts:"

  Part a: Starting with the right foot, do four triple steps forward.

  Part b: Rock weight forward on Count 1, then backward on Count 2, and add a CCW pivot turn on Counts 3, 4. During the pivot, keep your feet in a forward-backward stride position, lift your weight off your heels, and

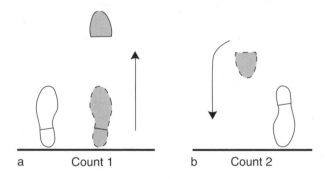

Figure 1.6   A CCW pivot makes a half turn.

turn on the balls of your feet to face the back wall. Make sure that you have transferred your weight forward onto your right foot then onto your left foot, giving each action one count (see Figure 1.6).

Student Option

- "Start the dance with your left foot. Notice what happens to your pivot turn (it now is a CW half turn)."

Student Keys to Success

- Maintain rhythm on both parts.

Student Success Goal

- Consecutive repetition of this two-part sequence for the length of one 4/4-time song.

To Decrease Difficulty

- Slow down the pivot turn to ensure that all actions (and weight shifts) occur with the counts.

To Increase Difficulty

- Eliminate the rock steps and immediately execute the pivot turn (making Part b only two counts).
- Reduce the number of repetitions in Part a to only two triple steps.

- Reduce the number of repetitions in Part a to only one triple step forward, then, in Part b to only two rock steps (forward and backward). Now, reverse for the second half: one triple step backward and two rock steps (backward and forward). [This is a lead-up to the cha-cha basic.]
- Reduce the number of repetitions in Part a to only one triple step forward, then, in Part b to one CW pivot turn. Now, reverse for the second half, one triple step forward (with left foot), and a CCW pivot turn. Notice that the pivot turns now alternate first CW (you will face front, then back), then CCW (you will face back, then front). [This is a lead-up to the cha-cha half chase.]

6. Electric Slide

Purpose and Organization

- Adding a quarter turn creates a four-wall dance, i.e., the dance starts over facing a new wall each time. It takes four repetitions to get back to the original front wall.
- Practice the sequence facing one wall until it is mastered. Gradually add a second repetition facing the second wall (side wall). Then add the third repetition facing the third wall (back wall), and finally the fourth repetition facing the fourth wall (side wall).
- This four-wall dance, called the "Electric Slide," works well to popular 4/4-time music. The original music, which has a nice, slow tempo, is titled "Electric Boogie," by Marcia Griffiths.

Instructions to Class

- "A four-wall dance requires a bit of orientation. Just remember that wherever your midline faces, it becomes your point of reference for moving left, right, forward, or backward."
- "In this four-wall dance, called the 'Electric Slide, Part a has a total of 12 counts (four counts in each of three different directions: right, left, and backward). Starting with your right foot, take three vine steps to your right (with a weight change on each step to the side, cross behind, and step to the side), and point your left toe on the fourth count. With your left foot free, take three vine steps (three weight changes to side, cross behind, to side) to your left, and point your right toe on the fourth count. The third direction is backward. Take three steps backward (RLR), and point your left toe forward on the fourth count."
- "Part b has a total of 6 counts (two counts in each of three directions). Step forward onto your left foot, and touch your right toe forward. Step backward onto your right foot, and touch your left toe forward. Rotate your left foot a quarter turn to your left (CCW) before you step onto your left foot, and scuff your right heel on the fourth count. Now you are facing a new wall, ready to start over again. Notice that this is the first time that we have done only one repetition to each direction, giving you less time to react."

Student Options

- "Substitute a travel turn during the three vine steps, or during the three walks backward."
- "Substitute slides to the sides. The rhythm is 'step-close, step-close, step-

close, step' or '1-and, 2-and, 3-and, 4.' Make sure your side step is on each whole count. Your movements can be controlled and low (feet touching the ground), or more in the air (like a gallop to the side). How vigorous do you want to be? It is up to you. When you are tired, you can go back to the vine steps."

- "Add a 1-1/4 turn instead of a quarter turn at the end of Part b. Just angle your left foot to face the next wall (making the quarter turn), and spin CCW quickly (adding a full turn)."
- "During the first four counts of Part b, you may add more actions, as follows: shimmy your shoulders; or touch the floor; or lean forward, then backward; or (if you are very agile) step forward onto your left foot, kneel on your right knee, and extend your left leg forward (bringing your right elbow back and your left arm forward, like a bow-and-arrow position)—all before your quarter turn to the left."

Student Keys to Success

- In Part a, group four counts in each of three directions: right, left, backward.
- In Part b, group two counts in each of three directions: forward, backward, quarter-turn left.

Student Success Goal

- Repeat this four-wall dance for the length of a 4/4-time song.

To Decrease Difficulty

- Practice each part separately, then together.
- Use slow counts, connecting each weight change or action with the counts.

To Increase Difficulty

- Increase the tempo of the music.
- Use a variety of musical styles.
- Include the student options.
- Ask students to add a quarter turn to any of the previous sequences to create a four-wall dance.

7. Circle Mixer

Purpose and Organization

- Because a mixer switches partners frequently, it is a fun way to introduce students to other classmembers, to get students dancing quickly without having to know much about technique, and to allow you the opportunity to informally observe your students' skill levels and have a better idea of where your students fit along the continuum of learning steps presented in this book.
- Set up students in a double circle with the leaders on the inside, the followers on the outside, and both facing the LOD (counterclockwise). Pair up to make couples. Position any singles in-between the couples (instead of letting them stand side-by-side) so that they will have a partner every other time the dance is repeated.
- After students know the mixer, ask them to introduce themselves to each new partner.
- Select slow to moderate 4/4-time music, e.g., popular music, or use a selection

from the *Swing* or *Fox-Trot Social Dance Music* audiocassettes. For variety, select folk songs (such as "Greensleeves") or country western music in 4/4 time.

Instructions to Class

- "This circle mixer groups four walking steps in four directions: forward, backward, diagonal left, and clockwise. Both partners start with the right foot."
- "In Part a (four counts), take three walking steps forward. On the fourth step, turn inward to face your partner."
- "In Part b (four counts), take three walking steps backward (away from your partner). On the fourth step, turn to face your diagonal left (facing CCW), which aligns you toward the next partner."
- "In Part c (four counts), take three walking steps on your own diagonal left toward your next partner (align right shoulders). On your fourth step, hook right elbows with your new partner."
- "In Part d (four counts), take three walks CW around your partner (with elbows

still hooked). On the fourth step, release elbows so that the follower can continue turning CW until both partners are facing the LOD again."

- "Repeat the entire dance with this new partner."

Student Options

- "Join inside hands during Part a."
- "Slap both palms with partner on the fourth count of Part a (when facing each other)."

Student Keys to Success

- Walk using a heel-ball-toe motion.
- Transfer weight onto the ball of each foot with each beat of the music.
- Align shoulders either perpendicular to the LOD (Part a), or parallel to your partner (Parts b, c, and d).

Student Success Goal

- Continuous repetition of the circle mixer for the length of one 4/4-time song.

To Decrease Difficulty

- Have students form a single circle, and practice the outside circle's parts without a partner. [This is a great aerobics routine.]
- Practice each part separately, gradually adding another part in an accumulative manner.

To Increase Difficulty

- Increase the tempo of the music.
- Use different locomotor movements (grouped in four counts), e.g., four skips (uneven rhythm), or two triple steps (uneven rhythm), or three walks and a hop (even rhythm), or combine two triple steps and two walks (intermixing uneven and even rhythm).

Summary

Line and patterned partner dances and mixers are fun ways to introduce, review, or informally assess your students' ability to transfer information to a new situation (the definition of learning). Select those drills and concepts that best fit your students' needs. Students can gain confidence and essential pre-requisite skills prior to learning the "packaged" basic steps, variations, and sequences presented in Steps 2-7 of this book. Additional mixers and potential dance situations that students may encounter in social settings are presented in Step 8.

Step 2 Introducing Basic Dance Steps and Short Combinations

There are universally accepted dance basics ("packaged" rhythmic patterns) for the fox-trot, waltz, cha-cha, swing, and polka. Wherever your students go to do these dances, they will find similar executions of these dance steps. Encourage students to add appropriate styling and flair while maintaining the correct execution of the basic steps. The eight basic steps (within five dance styles) covered in this book include one basic step each for the cha-cha, polka, and waltz, three basic steps for the swing (depending upon the tempo of the music), and two basic steps for the fox-trot (for box and magic rhythms).

Once students master the basic steps individually, they are ready to pair up with a partner. The six partner positions used within this book are organized according to the dance style in which they will be used. Nonverbal communication begins with knowing how to lead both into and out of the various partner positions (i.e., make transitions), how to signal a change in direction while executing the basic steps, and how to lead variations of the basic steps, such as a turn for the follower.

By the end of this instructor step, your students should be able to

- politely ask a partner to dance,
- combine at least four different leads, and
- demonstrate proper floor etiquette.

Use the material in this step for short units (i.e., 3 to 8 weeks) that focus on getting students started and practicing on the dance floor.

THREE INTERACTING VARIABLES

As you teach the basic steps for these dances, be aware that there are at least three interacting variables—the beat, the rhythm, and the footwork—all of which merge into a rhythmic pattern that can be repeated for the length of a song. These variables may be confusing to beginning dancers. For example, the polka step (initially introduced as the triple step in the previous step) involves three weight changes (counted as 1-and-2) within two beats

of music, and a fourth action, the hop, that occurs prior to the first count. As another example, there are three weight changes in the waltz (counted as 1, 2, 3) that occur within three beats of music. Let students know that their footwork (i.e., foot actions and weight changes) either will correspond exactly to the number of beats per measure (i.e., either one weight change or nonweight change occurs per beat of the music in even rhythms) or will correspond to only certain beats per measure (i.e., either fewer or more footwork actions than actual beats per measure may be taken within uneven rhythms). For example, avoid saying "1, 2, 3" when the timing is uneven, which is cued as "1-and-2." The former method gives the false impression that each footwork action or weight change gets one count. The latter method tells students that they will need to modify the timing of their footwork actions and weight changes (making three actions within two beats of music).

Because there is so much to attend to in the early stages of learning, it is helpful for students to become aware of those cues that are more reliable than others. The beat is usually constant while both the rhythm (reflected in the lyrics of the song) and the number of footwork actions are less reliable cues. Once the tempo of the basic step is established, it will usually be repeated for the length of the song. Use a consistent tempo when cuing the counts, and select music with consistent tempos.

GROUPING INFORMATION TO MAKE LEARNING EASIER

Instead of teaching the beat, footwork, and rhythm in isolation, emphasize their interaction as soon as possible. Show how they fit together to make the whole (in this case, a basic step or a rhythmic pattern). The three strategies used in this book reflect one way of grouping information to show how the footwork may be modified to match the beat of the music. Feel free to use other strategies that you feel accomplish the same goal—

grouping information first to show the commonalities, then to highlight the differences. Three selected strategies follow.

Footwork Strategy #1: Combine two locomotor movements.

Footwork Strategy #2: Alter the timing.

Footwork Strategy #3: Match an action with each beat or whole count of the music.

The order of these strategies assumes that students have had experience with even rhythms and uneven rhythms, in that order (see drills in Step 1). If not, start with Strategy #3 when working with your students. However, following a particular strategy order is not as important as sharing commonalities that can help students group and reference information (instead of learning isolated, unrelated parts). It is less cumbersome (and less intimidating) for students to learn *three* footwork strategies (types of basics) instead of *eight* basics (across five dance styles), each having multiple subparts. At the same time that you share similarities with your students, introduce the differences. Even though some of the basic steps may be comprised of the same locomotor movements—or use the same timing or rhythm—each should look different! Therefore, begin to include the styling aspects that give each dance style its unique character (see the first drill for each dance style later in this step).

Footwork Strategy #1: Combine Two Locomotor Movements

The footwork for three basic dance steps combine two locomotor movements: a triple step (also called a *step, ball change*) with one other locomotor movement (either two walks or a hop). These dance steps are the triple-lindy (swing) basic, the cha-cha basic, and the polka basic. The specific number of repetitions, order, and timing for each follow on page 26. You may verbally cue your students by calling out the footwork or the "Quick" (Q) and "Slow" (S) portions of the rhythmic pattern, or the counts. Vary your verbal cues and en-

courage your students to focus on those cues that help them best.

Footwork Strategy #2: Alter the Timing

The footwork for two basic dance steps uses one walking step within two beats of music. This timing modification occurs within the fox-trot and the single-lindy (swing) basic. The specific number of repetitions, order, and timing for each follow on page 26.

Footwork Strategy #3: Match an Action With Each Beat or Whole Count

The footwork for three basic dance steps uses either a weight change or a nonweight change (action) with each beat of the music. This occurs within the fox-trot box step (also called the "Westchester" box), the waltz box step, and the double-lindy (swing) basic. Notice that the step pattern for the fox-trot and the waltz box steps are the same (forward, side, close), yet the beats per measure are different (4/4 and 3/4 time, respectively). In order to help students be more aware of the timing and to introduce early styling differences, this book *purposely* places the fox-trot box step within footwork strategy #3 by adding a nonweight action during the "slow"—in order to give students something to do on each beat of the measure—for four counts. You may also include it under footwork strategy #2, *if* you do not emphasize the styling action of bringing the feet together (no weight change) prior to the side, close steps, which makes a sharp, 90-degree floor path. The specific number of repetitions, order, and timing for each follow on page 26.

BASIC PARTNER POSITIONS

There are six basic partner positions (see Figure 2.1a-f) used in the variations within this book. Whether students execute the basic steps in a traditional or in a modified version of these positions, it is helpful to orientate them to working with a partner early in the learning process.

Footwork Strategy #1

BASIC STEP	FOOTWORK	RHYTHMIC PATTERN	COUNTS
Triple-Lindy Swing (slow tempo)	• Triple step • Triple step • Ball, change	• QQS ♪♪♩ • QQS ♪♪♩ • QQ ♩♩	• 1-and-2 • 3-and-4 • 5, 6
Cha-Cha	• Break step • Triple step	• SS ♩♩ • QQS ♪♪♩	• 1, 2 [or 2, 3] • 3-and-4 [or 4-and-1]
Polka	• Hop • Triple step	• One-sixteenth note ♪ • QQS ♪♪♩	• a • 1-and-2

Footwork Strategy #2

BASIC STEP	FOOTWORK	RHYTHMIC PATTERN	COUNTS
Magic Step	• Walking step • Walking step • Side step • Close	• S ♩ • S ♩ • Q ♩ • Q ♩	• 1-2 • 3-4 • 5 • 6
Single-Lindy Swing (fast tempo)	• Walking step • Walking step • Ball • Change	• S ♩ • S ♩ • Q ♩ • Q ♩	• 1-2 • 3-4 • 5 • 6

Footwork Strategy #3

BASIC STEP	FOOTWORK	RHYTHMIC PATTERN	COUNTS
Fox-Trot Box (Westchester box)	• Walking step (weight change) • Brush free foot (non-weight change) • Side step • Close feet (weight change)	• "Sl-" } • "-ow" } ♩ • Q ♩ • Q ♩	• 1-2 • 3 • 4
Waltz Box	• Walking step (weight change) • Side step (weight change) • Close feet (weight change)	• S ♩ • S ♩ • S ♩	• 1 (accent) • 2 • 3
Double-Lindy Swing (moderate tempo)	• Dig toe • Drop heel (weight change) • Dig toe • Drop heel (weight change) • Ball • Change	• Q ♩ • Q ♩ • Q ♩ • Q ♩ • Q ♩ • Q ♩	• 1 • 2 • 3 • 4 • 5 • 6

a Shine position

b Two-hands joined (facing)

c One-hand joined (facing)

d Inside-hands joined

e Closed

f Semi-open

Figure 2.1 Six basic partner positions.

Detecting and Correcting Basic Partner Position Errors

You can help students improve their nonverbal communication for proper leading and following by checking that they are starting and moving within the proper partner position. Each partner needs to establish his or her personal space that is halfway to the other partner. Usually, the arms are curved, with the palms facing downward, and positioned in front of the shoulders. If students cannot see their hands with their peripheral vision, then they have opened their arms too wide.

Look for a frame (hand, wrist, elbow, and shoulder connection) between partners. For example, in the closed position, if the leader shifts weight forward, then the follower should also shift weight back (instead of letting the elbows collapse and allowing the partner to plow into the follower). You can intercept potential arguments by observing and correcting basic partner position errors, such as the following.

ERROR

CORRECTION

1. Students' arms are either very rigid or very limp (called spaghetti arms). In Error a, the follower has broken (lost) her frame by letting her right elbow bend. In Error b, the leader has also lost his frame by bending his left elbow and moving his torso forward.

1. Stand beside the couple and gently connect their arms to form a circle (imagine a beach ball in-between). From a closed dance position, ask the follower to wait until the leader's body weight has shifted onto the balls of his feet. The range of movement will be very slight, yet it is important for the follower to not move until the lead to move forward has been given (otherwise, the leader does not get a chance to learn how to lead; rather, he relies on the follower). Sometimes you may want to dance with each partner to show them the amount of force actually used to define one's own space. Ask students to think of keeping arms and shoulders connected and maintaining the distance in-between.

a ERROR: Follower's right elbow extends behind her shoulders.

b ERROR: Leader's left elbow extends behind his shoulders.

CORRECT: Maintain elbow, hand, and shoulder position when moving forward.

ERROR 🚫

CORRECTION

2. Students pump their arms in time with the rhythm.

2. An upper torso lean would be appropriate styling within the first four counts of the swing basics. Yet, it would greatly detract within the upright torso styling of the foxtrot, waltz, cha-cha, and polka, which are considered smooth dances. Ask students to feel that their energy is being pulled in the direction of the particular dance (e.g., forward, backward, or in the LOD) through their center of gravity.

3. Students let their elbows fully extend during either the one- or two-hands joined positions.

3. Ask students to stay within a smaller circle with their partner. They can imagine that their elbows are like shock absorbers that only let the elbows move 45 degrees either in front of or behind the vertical. Another potential error to watch for is whether either partner is taking too large of a back step during their ball-change or actually stepping flat-footed instead of placing the weight only on the ball of the foot within a few inches to a half step behind the heel of the other foot.

ERROR: Both partner's arms straighten, which places them too far apart and off-balance.

CORRECT: With elbows slightly bent, each partner's center of gravity is placed over the feet, which improves balance as well as leading and following.

GENERAL TEACHING PROCEDURES TO FACILITATE STUDENT PRACTICE

Regardless of the number of dances that you select to teach in your dance unit, there are general teaching procedures that you can follow and modify to best fit your situation. When introducing a new basic, work it until students have success with it and its variations. The following general teaching procedures are applied for each dance style in the drill sections in this book:

1. Practice basic alone (without a partner).
2. Practice basic in a modified partner position (such as facing the partner with fingertips touching) or in a position relative to a partner without touching.
3. Practice basic in a specific partner position (such as closed position or semi-open position).
4. Add a turn.
5. Practice in a performance context. Consecutively repeat the basic to music while applying good floor etiquette with a partner (whether doing a LOD or spot dance, in order to get an orientation to the flow of traffic and to learn how to adjust leads to avoid collisions with other couples).
6. Combine up to four leads within a sequence, with a partner, and set to music.

RHYTHMIC CONCEPTS: STUDENT KEYS TO SUCCESS

Use the drills in this step to introduce your students to however many basic steps (eight within five dance styles are provided) that you wish to include in your dance unit. The following list of concepts assumes all five dance styles are being included.

1. *"Slow" and "quick" cues reflect a 2:1 relative ratio.* The "slow" is twice as long as the "quick." The tempo (speed of execution) may vary between songs, yet it will usually be constant within most songs. (For your beginners, remember to select music that has a consistent tempo.)

2. *Be aware of the amount of space used in each dance, whether LOD or spot.* Dances that travel in a counterclockwise direction around the perimeter of the floor (whenever there are no other couples in the immediate path) include the polka, waltz, and fox-trot. Dances that

remain stationary in a small, circular area include the swing and the cha-cha. LOD dances may mix traveling variations and stationary variations, as necessary, to avoid collisions.

3. *Use a two-repetition minimum "rule" before changing to another basic or variation.* Using this rule early in the learning process gives both partners more time to adjust. The leader may do more than two repetitions. Once students can react more quickly and do not need extra thinking time to decide what to do next, this rule may be eliminated.

4. *Select the appropriate basic that best fits the music.* Some musical selections are more obvious, such as a waltz, cha-cha, or a polka, than others. Sometimes the swing and fox-trot may be danced to the same music selection. If so, it is important to follow good floor etiquette and set up within the center of the room for spot dances (such as the swing) or to follow the LOD for traveling dances (such as the fox-trot).

5. *Select the appropriate swing basic according to the tempo of music.* If the tempo is slow, do the triple-lindy swing basic. If the tempo is fast, do the single-lindy swing basic. If the tempo is in-between these extremes, do the double-lindy swing basic.

Introducing Swing Basics

The swing, an American dance that evolved from the jazz era of the 1920s, was first known as the jitterbug. The early jitterbug steps were inspired by boogie-woogie music and had a "slow, slow, quick, quick" rhythmic pattern that is still used today. Later, the "Lindy Hop" was introduced in honor of Charles Lindbergh's 1927 transatlantic solo flight. In time, the "Lindy Hop" became known simply as the lindy. When syncopated rock-and-roll music was introduced during the late 1940s, the double lindy became popular.

Today, there are three popular lindy variations: single, double, and triple. Each refers to the actual number of steps taken during the "slow, slow" portions of the rhythmic pattern. Encourage students to select the most appropriate basic according to the tempo of the music. If the tempo is slow, use the triple lindy. If the tempo is fast, use the single lindy. If the tempo is moderate, use the double lindy. Dancers often have a personal preference when choosing which lindy variation to use. Partners need not execute the same lindy variation at the same time.

This section introduces the swing basics in two partner positions: semiopen and one-hand joined. Step 3 will add variation and partner position options.

PRESENTATION ORDER

Because the three lindy variations each use a different footwork strategy, you have at least three options as to what order to introduce them to your students. If you want to present the easiest variation to learn first, then start with the double lindy pattern because it corresponds one foot action with each beat of the music (Footwork Strategy #3). If you want to stress the tempo of the music (slow, moderate, fast), then start with the triple lindy because it gives students more response time to get eight footwork actions within six beats of music (Footwork Strategy #1). If you want to stress the number of foot actions in a chronological order (one, two, or three for single, double, and triple lindy variations, respectively), then start with the single lindy because it uses one weight change with two beats of music during the "slow, slow" portion (Footwork Strategy #2). Whatever order you select, let students know the relationship among these three lindy variations.

EXECUTION AND STYLING

All three lindy variations within the swing are executed within a spot on the floor that is approximately 5 to 10 feet in diameter. You may start students from a variety of partner positions. However, this book both starts and ends students within the semiopen position for three reasons. First, the feet may be placed either (a) parallel with the lead foot slightly ahead of the trailing foot, which facilitates the use of the directional cues "forward, backward" on the "slow, slow" portion or (b) with the heel of the lead foot at the instep of the other foot, which is a foot position styling point (modified third position in ballet) used within many of the later swing variations. Figure 2.2 shows the semiopen position and the swing's unique hand grip with the man's thumb on top. Second, the swing is a rotational dance in that both partners constantly

rotate either CW or CCW within their staked-out spot. Executing swing variations from a stationary position slows down the flow, which is helpful in early learning. In later learning stages, students enjoy the challenge of moving, which is more exciting. Third, students more easily remember not only the individual variations, but also when to use the variations when they are categorized by different partner positions—making a closed loop sequence. If you prefer to start (and end) your students with either a one- or two-hands joined position, then watch that students take small sideward steps (they have a tendency to take very wide side steps), and encourage students to swivel on the balls of their feet prior to each "slow," giving them more body action and facilitating smaller steps. Notice that the same closed-loop concept applies—it's just a matter of where the students begin (and end).

Figure 2.2   Suggested semiopen starting position for the swing.

Be prepared to recognize and modify your instructions to fit at least two student skill levels: beginning and accomplished. Note that the beginning student responses reflect typical errors while the accomplished student responses reflect the desired execution and styling. Use the technique and styling criteria within the following rating chart in either an informal or a formal way to assess proper execution and styling of the basic lindy variations.

Lindy Technique and Styling Rating Chart

CRITERION	BEGINNING	ACCOMPLISHED
Semiopen Position	• Stands side by side partner, or faces partner • Weight on both heels	• Angles feet and body 45 degrees toward partner • Stand on inside foot with heel of outside foot slightly off the floor (ready position)
Execution a. **During "slow, slow"** • **Triple Lindy** • **Double Lindy** • **Single Lindy** b. **During "quick, quick"**	• Three large steps • Equal timing • Heel-ball-toe on each step • Feet pass during triple steps • Flat-footed steps • Immediate weight shifts from one foot to the other • Shifts weight back on heel • Inside foot remains on floor (no weight change)	• Three small steps • First and second step quicker • Only ball of foot on "and" • One foot leads during triple steps • Dig toe, then drop heel • Slight knee bend added at end of each weight change • Weight change onto the ball of the outside foot (positioned close to the heel of the inside foot) • Inside foot lifts and lowers (weight change) in same location (flat-footed action)
Styling a. **During "slow, slow"** b. **During "quick, quick"**	• Torso erect • Upper torso leans back	• Torso and outside shoulder lean slightly in direction of movement • Upper torso remains over base (feet)

Drills for Short Swing Combinations

1. Lindy Techniques—In-Place Leads

Purpose and Organization

- Students' confidence levels will increase as they demonstrate each basic step (a) alone to counts (without music), then with slow music, and (b) with a partner to counts (without music), then with a partner to slow music.
- Use a scattered formation, separating the room in half for each part in order to give students an orientation to their partner's position: Leaders on the left side, and followers on the right side (initially assuming a nontouching, semiopen position).
- A triangle image helps orientate students to their relationship with a partner (see Figure 2.3).

Instructions to Class

- "The three lindy basics share three commonalities: (a) six total counts, (b) the direction of movement for foot placement is forward, backward, backward, then forward (in semiopen position), and (c) the styling is jazzy and syncopated with a torso lean during the 'slow, slow' rhythmic cues and upright during the 'quick, quick' rhythmic cues."
- "The number of footwork actions used within the 'slow, slow' rhythmic cues varies according to the tempo of the music: three footwork actions with a slow tempo, two footwork actions with a moderate tempo, and one footwork action with a fast tempo."

Triple-Lindy Basic

Figure 2.4 shows the basic triple-lindy footwork. Review note values on page 26.

- *Footwork:* Triple step, triple step (six weight changes), ball change (two weight changes)

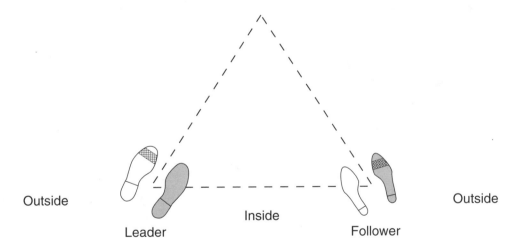

Outside   Inside   Outside

Leader   Follower

Figure 2.3 A triangle image helps orientate partners in semiopen position.

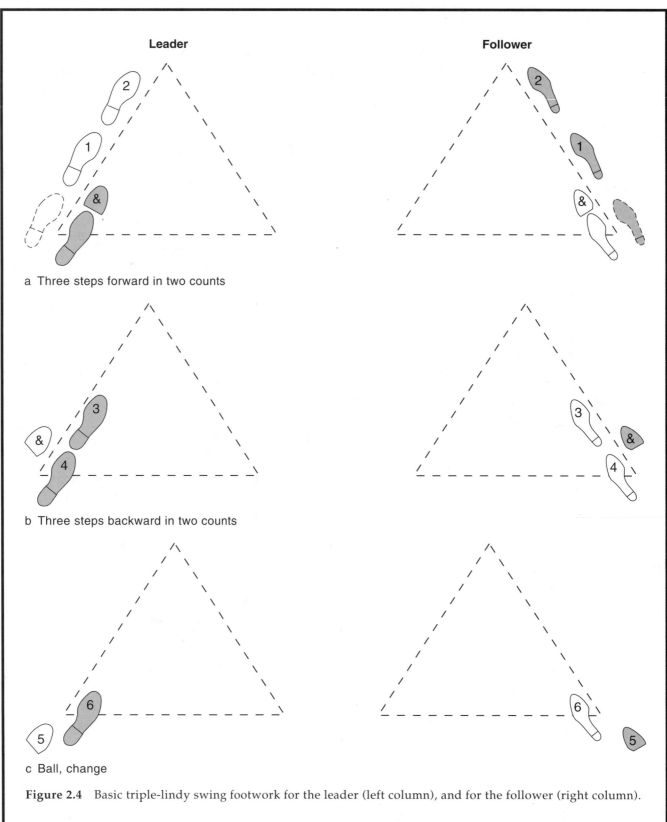

Leader   **Follower**

a Three steps forward in two counts

b Three steps backward in two counts

c Ball, change

Figure 2.4   Basic triple-lindy swing footwork for the leader (left column), and for the follower (right column).

- *Rhythmic pattern:* QQS, QQS, QQ
- *Counts:* 1-and-2, 3-and-4, 5, 6

Double-Lindy Basic

Figure 2.5 shows the double-lindy footwork.

- *Footwork:* Dig toe, drop heel (weight change), dig toe, drop heel (weight change), ball-change (two weight changes)
- *Rhythm:*   QQ, QQ, QQ
- *Counts:* 1, 2, 3, 4, 5, 6

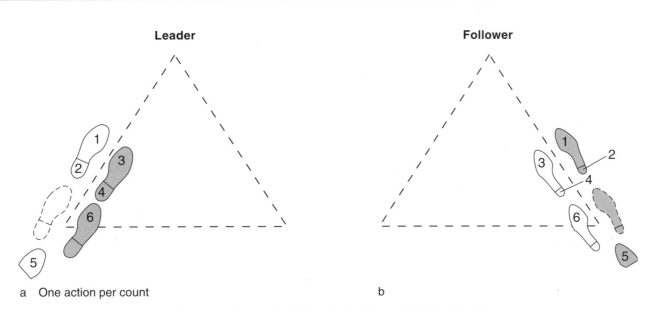

a   One action per count   b

Figure 2.5   Basic double-lindy swing footwork (a) for the leader, and (b) for the follower.

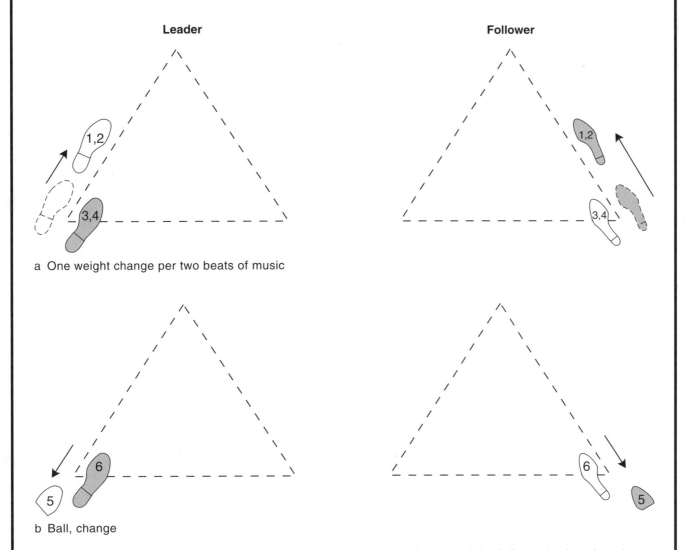

a One weight change per two beats of music

b Ball, change

Figure 2.6   Basic single-lindy swing footwork for the leader (left column) and the follower (right column).

Single-Lindy Basic

Figure 2.6 shows the basic single-lindy footwork.

- *Footwork:* Four weight changes
- *Rhythm:* SSQQ
- *Counts:* 1-2, 3-4, 5, 6

Student Success Goal

- Competently demonstrate basic steps alone, to counts, to music, then with a partner in semiopen position, to counts, and to music.

To Decrease Difficulty

- Isolate the subparts, then gradually accumulate them, making sure that the students both understand and can demonstrate the proper foot actions with the proper counts.

- Use a modified partner position with partners gently touching fingertips.
- Stress the imaginary triangle on the floor that connects both partners within the semiopen position: The leader stands in left corner, and the follower stands in right corner; both partners' feet and bodies are angled 45 degrees toward the top of the triangle.

To Increase Difficulty

- Either progress the students more quickly through the general practice procedures, or, start them in semiopen position.
- Ask couples to stay within their own "spot" (instead of facing the same wall) and to avoid bumping into others.

2. Add CW and CCW Rotation Leads

Purpose and Organization

- This drill will help students get a feel for the fun of revolving with a partner as well as prepare them to later execute variations while revolving within their spot.
- Set up rows of partners in semiopen position, facing the same wall.

Instructions to Class

- "Ultimately, the swing variations are executed while revolving with a partner within your spot. You may rotate either CW or CCW."
- "There are two strong leads that occur between the ball change steps. Whether rotating CW or CCW, the leader will gently push with one hand and pull with the other after the "ball," which signals the follower to angle her inside foot in the direction of the desired rotation. During the "change," the leader needs to keep his arms firm within the semiopen position (resisting the rotation), if he wants his partner to say in place. He may, however, facilitate the rotation and only

make his arms firm when he wants to stop rotating."

Student Success Goal

- Competently demonstrate both CW and CCW rotations with a partner in semiopen position to music.

To Decrease Difficulty

- Ask students gradually to increase the degree of rotation during the ball change. For example, they might take four to eight basic steps within a full rotation, increasing the degree of each turn (from an eighth to a quarter turn) per basic. As they transfer weight on the "change," they will be facing a new direction and can start the basic again.

To Increase Difficulty

- Encourage students to rotate not only on the ball change, but also on the "slow, slow" portion as well, which will greatly increase the degree of rotation (perhaps getting a full rotation within only one or two basics). They need to keep the momentum going.

3. Two Transition Leads

Purpose and Organization

- This drill gives students two ways of moving both into and out of another partner position, in this case from a semiopen position "out" to a one-hand joined position, than back "in" to a semiopen position. Notice that a closed-loop cycle occurs (drills within Step 3 of this book will expand this cycle).
- If you have not already introduced the image of an imaginary triangle on the floor, it will be helpful to do so in this drill to encourage proper rotation.
- Set up rows of partners in semiopen position, facing the same wall.

Instructions to Class

- "Two sets of transitions may be used to take you from a semiopen position into a one-hand joined position, and then back again to a semiopen position: an arch-out and an arch-in, and a roll-out and a roll-in."
- "The follower's timing is the same in both options, even though the directions change."
- "The leads for the first set involve vertical arm actions while the leads for the second set are more horizontal."

Arch-Out and Arch-In

- *On Count 6:* The leader lifts his left hand and arm to form an arch with his partner.
- *At the end of first "slow" cue:* The leader gently presses the heel of his right hand on the follower's left shoulder blade (see Figure 2.7a). The follower spins 180 degrees CW to face the man.
- *On the second "slow" cue:* Both partners face each other (see Figure 2.7b).
- *On Count 6:* The leader lifts his left hand and arm to form another arch with his partner.
- *At the end of the first "slow" cue:* The leader makes a small CCW circular motion above the follower's head to signal a CCW 180-degree turn back under the arch (see Figure 2.7c).
- *On Count 5:* The leader places his right arm on the follower's left shoulder blade to resume a semiopen position.

Roll-Out and Roll-In

- *On Count 6:* The leader initiates a sweep of his right arm and shoulder toward his left-diagonal front direction.
- *At the end of the first "slow" cue:* The leader continues his right arm extension. The

a Arch-out   b One-hand position   c Arch-in

Figure 2.7 Arch-out and arch-in transitions out of and back to the semiopen position.

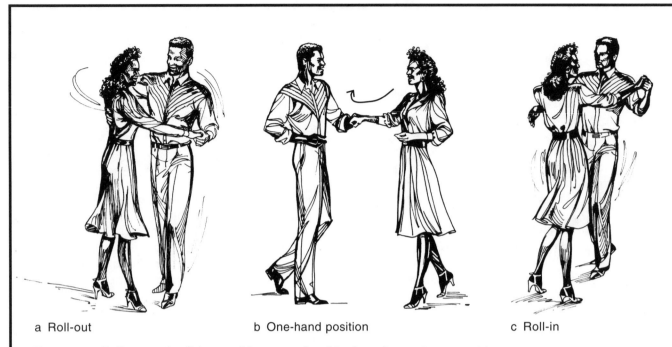

a Roll-out   b One-hand position   c Roll-in

Figure 2.8   Roll-out and roll-in transitions out of and back to the semiopen position.

follower spins 180 degrees CCW to face the leader (see Figure 2.8a).

- *On the second "slow" cue:* Both partners face each other (see Figure 2.8b).
- *On Count 6:* The leader gently pulls his left hand toward his right side.
- *At the end of the first "slow" cue:* The leader makes a horizontal CW circular motion (tracing a "J" horizontally with his left hand) to signal a CW 180-degree turn for the follower (see arrow in Figure 2.8b).
- *On Count 5:* The leader places his right arm on the follower's left shoulder blade to resume a semiopen position (see Figure 2.8c).

Student Success Goal

- Competently demonstrate the arch-out, arch-in, roll-out, and roll-in transitions from a semiopen position to a one-hand joined position, and back to a semiopen position.

To Decrease Difficulty

- Use the concept of an imaginary triangle on the floor (or you can place tape on the floor) to show the interrelationship between both partners' locations. Set up beside a partner without touching hands (leader on left, follower on right), and

have both angle 45 degrees inward to face the top of the triangle. Without doing the basics, ask students to shift their locations first CCW, then CW. Thus, the follower moves to the top of the triangle and faces the corner she vacated as the leader moves to the right corner of the triangle (taking the follower's vacated starting location) and faces the top of the triangle (where his partner is standing). Then, reverse directions to get back to the original locations (the leader moves back to the left side, while the follower moves back to the right side of the triangle).

- Isolate the follower's half turn without a partner (spin 180 degrees on the ball of the right foot). Practice both CW and CCW 180-degree spins. Use the appropriate basic, and time the spin to occur at the end of the first "slow."
- Because both transition leads serve the same purpose, you may decide to teach only one set of them.

To Increase Difficulty

- Let students know that they have the option to intermix transition leads. For example, they might do an arch-out and a roll-in, or vice versa.

4. Combine Four Leads

Purpose and Organization

- This drill helps students identify the decision-making options that the leader has when combining at least four different leads to create a short sequence.
- Let students stake out their own spots.

Instructions to Class

- "You know how to do the basic lindy in place, how to rotate CW and CCW, and how to transition two partner positions with an arch-out and an arch-in, or a roll-out and a roll-in."
- "An easy way to remember all these options is to start to cluster them together. Experiment with different ways of combining at least four leads with a partner in order to create a short sequence. You may repeat any number of basics between each lead."

Student Success Goal

- Competently demonstrate at least four short sequences that combine at least four leads.

To Decrease Difficulty

- Provide students with specific suggestions for solving this task, such as the following:
  - a. In-place basics, CW rotation, arch-out, arch-in
  - b. In-place basics, CCW rotation, in-place basics, CW rotation
  - c. CCW rotation, roll-out, roll-in, in-place basics
  - d. CCW rotation, roll-out, arch-in, CW rotation

To Increase Difficulty

- Ask students to repeat each short sequence at least twice.
- Let those students who want to demonstrate their favorite sequences do so for the rest of the class.
- Have students repeat this drill with different partners. Use a musical chair approach so that each time you stop the music, students need to quickly find another partner.

Introducing Cha-Cha Basics

A popular Latin dance is the cha-cha, which was originally called the cha-cha-cha—in Cuba, during the mid-1950s—to reflect the three quick steps used in the footwork and the three calypso sounds heard in the music. Finding the three "chas" cumbersome, Americans shortened the name. The cha-cha is a blend of other dances. It has a rhythm similar to the mambo, styling similar to that of the rhumba, and footwork similar to the triple lindy.

This section introduces the cha-cha basic in three partner positions: shine, two-hands (and one-hand) joined, and closed. Step 4 will add variation options from these partner positions.

TWO RHYTHM CHOICES

There are two rhythm choices within the cha-cha: American or Latin. The choice is whether to initiate the break (or rock) step on the downbeat or the upbeat. The American version breaks on Count 1 (the downbeat), while the Latin version breaks on Count 2 (the upbeat). In a social setting, students will encounter the American rhythm, for example, within line dances. In a ballroom or competitive setting, your students will encounter the Latin rhythm. The American rhythm was widely taught in the 50's, 60's and 70's. However, the Latin rhythm has recently become popular in couples dancing. Because the counts and timing cues are different, it will be easier for students to remain with one cha-cha rhythm or the other instead of switching rhythms. Both rhythms are described in more detail within the first cha-cha drill. Select the most appropriate version both for your situation and for your students.

CUBAN MOTION

Although the ultimate styling feature of the cha-cha includes Cuban motion, you will find that both rhythm versions may or may not be executed with Cuban motion by your students. Cuban motion involves a delayed weight transfer from one leg to the other, which is often difficult for beginning students. Introduce Cuban motion whenever you feel that your students are ready for it.

The natural hip movement in Cuban motion results from keeping one leg straight and the other leg (knee) bent. Hips should not be thrust from side to side. In a teaching progression, ask students to place all their weight on one leg (with the opposite knee bent and nonweight bearing) and to alternate their weight (shift weight from one leg to the other, as if waiting on a friend who is late). Gradually have students combine the two actions: Position the inside of their nonweight-bearing foot on the floor at the exact instant that their weight settles onto the opposite hip. Use the cues "shift-and-place" (again, delay the weight shift until the exact instant that the foot is placed). Ask students to experiment with placing the nonweight-bearing foot in different directions: forward, backward, and sideward. The sideward Cuban motion steps are similar to the merengue basic steps (that is, moving the feet in a side, close manner). Stress very small steps.

EXECUTION AND STYLING

The cha-cha, like the swing, is a spot dance. Thus, students may stake out a spot on the floor that is approximately 5 to 10 feet in diameter and free from other couples.

The footwork for the American rhythm starts immediately into the break (or rock) step, while the footwork for the Latin rhythm starts with a side step, then moves into the break (or rock) step. Then, after this first step, the footwork is the same, only the direction of the break (or rock) step changes.

In the American rhythm, the leader breaks forward on Count 1, while in the Latin rhythm, the leader steps sideward on Count 1, and breaks backward on Count 2.

Be prepared to recognize and modify your instructions to fit at least two student skill levels: beginning and accomplished. Note that the beginning student responses reflect typical errors while the accomplished student responses reflect the desired execution and styling. Use the technique and styling criterion within the following rating chart in either an informal or a formal way to assess proper execution and styling of the basic cha-cha.

Cha-Cha Technique and Styling Rating Chart

CRITERION	BEGINNING	ACCOMPLISHED
Shine Position	• Arms hang at sides • Weight on both feet	• Arms flexed 90 degrees with elbows close to body, and palms facing down • Weight on one foot and on the ball of the starting foot (leader's left, follower's right)
Execution **a. During "slow, slow"** **b. During "quick, quick, slow"**	• One weight change with a touch • Middle step quicker, like a triple step	• Break steps involve two weight changes with feet in forward and backward stride • Equal timing with feet slightly passing
Styling	• Nonweight-bearing heel lifted higher than toe • Arms and hands hang	• Feet flat with weight on inside edges (foot flexed at ankle) and toes slightly out • Arms and hands "talk" (flow with the body's motion)

Drills for Short Cha-Cha Combinations

1. Cha-Cha Technique in Shine Position

Purpose and Organization

• The purpose of this drill is to introduce students to the basic footwork and styling for the cha-cha within a facing, nontouching (shine) position. You might use the analogy of a spotlight shining on each partner, especially when challenge variations (see next drill) are used.
• Both partners' parts are identical and may be taught at the same time.

• When facing a partner, the leader starts with the left foot, and the follower starts with the right foot.
• The rhythm version selected determines which direction each partner breaks in.

Instructions to Class

• "The cha-cha basic includes two halves (four counts per half). A rocking motion is used during the break step that shifts

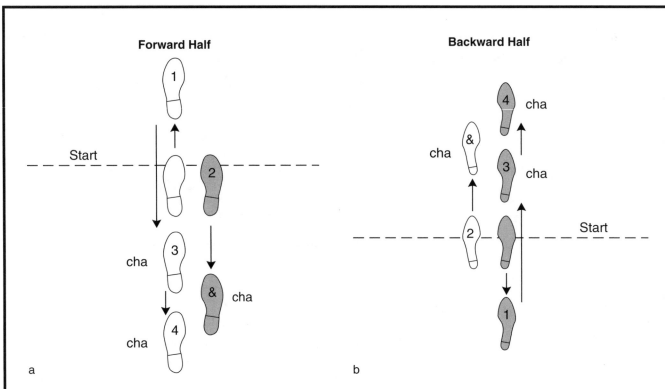

Figure 2.9   American rhythm cha-cha basic (a) for the leader, and (b) for the follower.

weight either forward-backward or backward-forward (depending upon which half is being executed). During the cha-cha-chas, the direction of movement for foot placement is either backward-backward-backward or forward-forward-forward (depending upon which half is being executed)."

American Rhythm Cues

- *Footwork:* Alternate a break step (two weight changes) and cha-cha-cha steps (three weight changes) (see Figure 2.9).
- *Rhythmic pattern:* SS, QQS
- *Counts:* 1, 2, 3-and-4

Latin Rhythm Cues

- *Footwork:* Take one side step, then alternate a break step (two weight changes) and cha-cha-cha steps (three weight changes) (see Figure 2.10).
- *Rhythmic pattern:* Side, SS, QQS
- *Counts:* Side (on Count 1), 2, 3, 4-and-1. (*Note:* The extra slow is only taken once,

whenever students start [or stop and start over].)

Student Success Goal

- Competently demonstrate basic step alone, to counts, to music, then with a partner in shine position, to counts, and to music.

To Decrease Difficulty

- Use a modified partner position with partners gently touching fingertips to get the feeling of moving in unison with a partner, i.e., as the leader moves forward, the follower moves backward, and vice versa. Then, in shine position, try it with "invisible strings" connecting partners, pulling them either forward or backward.

To Increase Difficulty

- Ask couples to stake out their own spot (instead of all facing the same direction) and to avoid bumping into other couples.

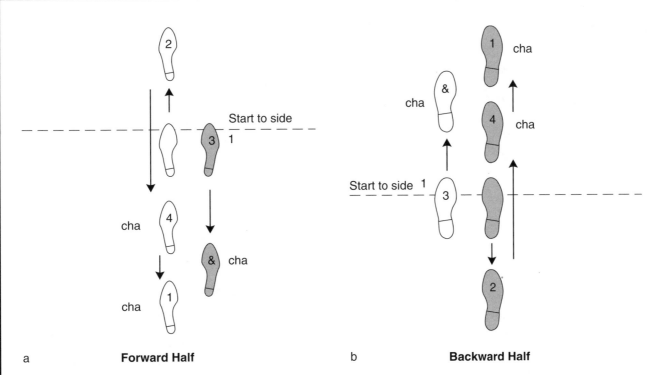

a   **Forward Half**   b   **Backward Half**

Figure 2.10   Latin rhythm cha-cha basic (a) for the follower, and (b) for the leader.

2. Half Chase

Purpose and Organization

- This drill has two purposes: to introduce a pivot (180 degree) turn and to practice styling points, including "talking" with the hands and flirting with the eyes.
- Set up rows of couples in shine position, with the leaders all facing the same direction.

Instructions to Class

- "It takes two half chases to complete a cycle with your partner. Both partners' footwork are the same, only the timing of when to do it differs. The leader initiates the chase, and the follower follows (four counts later)."
- "On any forward half basic, the leader places his left foot forward, pivots CW 180 degrees (shifting weight onto the right foot), then executes the forward cha-cha-chas (with his back to his partner). Simultaneously, while the follower's left foot is now free to repeat the leader's CW pivot, the leader places his right foot forward, pivots CCW 180 degrees (shifting weight onto the left foot), then executes the forward cha-cha-chas. The follower repeats the CCW pivot, too. To signal the end of the chase, the man remains facing his partner while executing forward and backward half basics."

- "Keep your elbows at approximately a 90-degree angle and close to the sides of your body. With palms facing downward, let your arms and hands rotate and move freely; "talk" with your hands. Look over your left shoulder as long as you can before your CW pivot turn is completed, then look over your right shoulder as long as you can before your CCW pivot turn is completed. This is a way of flirting with your eyes to challenge each other to continue the chase."

Student Success Goal

- Competently demonstrate the half chase alone, to counts, to music, then with a partner in shine position, to counts, and to music.

To Decrease Difficulty

- Freeze students' positions on both counts of the pivot turn. Watch for a tendency to rotate the left toe (in a pigeon-toed position) instead of keeping it parallel, and check that the weight has been shifted onto the right foot at the end of the CW 180-degree turn (instead of keeping weight on the left foot). Then, check that the weight has been shifted onto the left foot at the end of the CCW 180-degree turn (instead of keeping weight on the right foot).

To Increase Difficulty

- Ask the leader to do more than two half chases in a row (using any multiple of two). The follower should continue responding with half chases until the leader remains facing the original direction.

3. Transition to Two Hands

Purpose and Organization

- This drill shows students how to connect two partner positions: from a shine position to a two-hands joined position and back to a shine position. The direction of movement remains forward and backward.
- Set up rows of partners in shine position, with the leaders all facing the same wall.

Instructions to Class

- "From a shine position, the leader may move (transition) to a two-hands joined position during any forward-traveling cha-cha-chas (or, right, left, right footwork). Merely close up the space between partners, and place the thumbs under the follower's downward facing palms. His fingers gently lower on top of the follower's hand (see Figure 2.11)."
- "Once in a two-hands joined position, the leader gently presses forward (or pulls back slightly) just at the end of the break step."
- "To get back to a shine position, the leader releases his grasp during his backward-traveling cha-cha-chas (left, right, left footwork), opening up the space in-between."

Student Success Goal

- Competently demonstrate the transition from a shine position to a two-hands joined position, and back to a shine position, to music.

To Decrease Difficulty

- Use a set number of basics throughout, for example, four basics in shine position, four basics in two-hands joined position, and four basics in shine position.

To Increase Difficulty

- Let students do any even-number of basics within each partner position, keeping in mind the goal of completing a smooth transition.

Figure 2.11 Leader's cha-cha hand position in the two-hands joined position.

4. Basic "H" Floor Pattern

Purpose and Organization

- This drill shows students how to execute a basic "H" floor pattern from a closed dance position, adding a new direction of travel (sideward). Numerous variations are possible from this basic floor pattern (described in Step 4).
- Pair partners in rows, in closed position with leaders all facing the same wall.

Instructions to Class

- "Imagine an 'H' shape on the floor (see Figure 2.12). During your break steps, you will be moving forward and backward (along the vertical axis), while during your cha-cha-chas, you will be moving sideward (along the horizontal)."

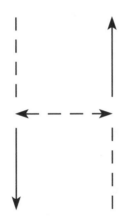

Figure 2.12 Basic "H" floor pattern.

- "From a closed position, the leader keeps his right hand firm during the break steps, then gently presses with the heel of his right hand (or pulls with his fingertips) to signal the sideward movements."

Student Success Goal

- Competently demonstrate the basic "H" floor pattern alone, to counts, to music, then with a partner in closed position, to counts, and to music.

To Decrease Difficulty

- Have students face each other without touching (to get a feel for the direction changes), then ask them to lightly touch fingertips.
- Either put tape on the floor (remember to remove it), or identify an existing line on the floor for students to travel on during the sideward movements (tendency is to travel on a diagonal during the cha-cha-chas, which will confuse the follower to anticipate forward-backward travel).

To Increase Difficulty

- Have students start in shine position, move into closed position (as they did with the two-hands joined position), and back to shine position.

5. Side Breaks

Purpose and Organization

- This drill introduces a side break and two ways of moving (making transitions) from one partner position to another. The starting position may be either a two-hands joined position or a closed position, then you'll move to a one-hand joined position (when facing each side).
- Either starting position combines four leads that move partners in four directions: forward, backward, and sideward.

Instructions to Class

- "Until now, you have been doing your break steps in a forward or backward direction. The break steps may also be executed to the side. Try it from two different starting positions; the leads are also different from each starting position."

From a Two-Hands Joined Position

- "During the leader's forward traveling cha-cha-chas (right, left, right footwork), he releases his right hand and slowly brings his left hand and arm across his midline. The break steps are executed facing the leader's right side. Resume a two-hands joined position and face your partner with shoulders and hips parallel during the sideward cha-cha-chas. Then release one hand to open to the other side on the break steps (see Figure 2.13)."

- "The leader may lead any even number of side break steps before either releasing hands to move to shine position, or grasping both hands and pressing forward during the sideward cha-cha-chas."

Figure 2.13 Cha-cha break position to the leader's left side.

From a Closed Position

- "Start with the basic 'H' pattern. Anytime during the leader's right, sideward-traveling cha-cha-chas (right, left, right footwork), he may release his right hand, let more space in-between, and bring his left hand and arm across his midline. This opens both partners to the side for the side breaks (two weight changes) in a one-hand joined position. Then, face each other (with shoulders and hips parallel) as the leader regrasps both hands during the sideward cha-cha-chas, and he releases his left hand to open both partners toward the other side (see Figure 2.13."

- "To get back into a closed position, do one more side break (to leader's right side). Then, the leader retains his left hand grasp and places his right hand on the follower's left shoulder blade, during the sideward cha-cha-chas. Continue the basic 'H' pattern in closed position."

Student Success Goals

- Competently demonstrate the transition from a two-hands joined position to a one-hand joined position (side break), then back to a two-hands joined position, to music.
- Competently demonstrate the transition from a closed position to a one-hand joined position (side break), then back to a closed position, to music.

To Decrease Difficulty

- Make sure students master one transition option before learning the other option.

To Increase Difficulty

- Ask students to make a continuous cycle from one position to the next, including both starting positions at some point.

Introducing Polka Basics

The polka is a vigorous, fun dance that originated as a folk dance step found in Polish, English, and German folk dances. The styling of each varies, ranging from a light, springy quality to a heavy, forceful quality.

The goal in the polka is to travel in the LOD (CCW around the perimeter of the room) whenever progress is not blocked by other couples. Couples may start from a variety of positions. This section introduces the polka basic in three partner positions: inside hands joined, semiopen position, and closed position. Step 5 will add variation options from these partner positions.

EXECUTION AND STYLING

The footwork for the polka blends a hop (see note values on page 26) and a triple step within two counts (one measure of 2/4 time). Because there are three footwork actions, the polka step is executed alternatively on each side of the body before students' starting foot is free again.

Be prepared to recognize and modify your instructions to fit at least two student skill levels: beginning and accomplished. Note that the beginning student responses reflect typical errors while the accomplished student responses reflect the desired execution and styling. Use the technique and styling criteria in the following rating chart in either an informal or formal way to assess the proper execution and styling of the basic polka.

Polka Technique and Styling Rating Chart

CRITERION	BEGINNING	ACCOMPLISHED
Inside-Hands Joined Position	• Man's palm faces back • Starting position weight distributed on both feet	• Man's palm faces front • Starting position weight on inside foot (closest to partner)
Execution a. **During "a"** b. **During "quick, quick, slow"**	• Hop is late, getting a half count or more • Body rises in the air during the triple step	• Hop occurs prior to the first beat in each measure, getting one-sixteenth of a beat • Head height remains level during the triple step (knees bend)
Styling	• Outside hand hangs at side	• Outside hand on hip

Drills for Short Polka Combinations

1. Polka Technique From an Inside-Hands Joined Position

Purpose and Organization

- The purpose of this drill is to introduce students to the basic footwork and styling for the polka. The direction of movement is LOD.
- Both parts are identical and may be taught at the same time.
- The starting position is an inside-hands joined position. The leaders start with the left foot and the followers start with the right foot.

Instructions to Class

- "The polka basic has two sides, a left and a right (or a right and a left, depending on which side you start). Each polka basic has four foot actions that need to be executed in two counts of music. Start with a hop (remember Newton's law of equal and opposite reaction, and bend your knee prior to pushing off, then land on the same foot). Do a triple step. On your last step, notice that your knee is already slightly bent. Take advantage of this bend to push off the floor into a hop, then do another triple step. Notice that your body moves vertically during the hop, then horizontally (forward) during the triple step."

Figure 2.14 shows the basic polka footwork.

- *Footwork:* A hop (bend, push off, rise mid-air, and land onto the same foot), then a triple step (three weight changes); repeat basic on both sides of the body.
- *Rhythmic pattern:* a-QQS; a-QQS
- *Counts:* a-1-and-2, a-3-and-4 (both sides of body); or, a-1-and-2; a-2-and-2; . . . (eight basics within a phrase of music)

Student Success Goal

- Competently demonstrate basic step alone, to counts, to music, then with a partner from an inside-hands joined position, to counts, and to music.

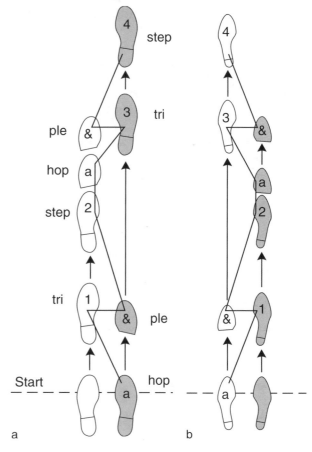

Figure 2.14   Basic polka footwork (a) for the leader, and (b) for the follower.

To Decrease Difficulty

- Isolate the parts within the basic, especially practicing a skip to give students a feel for the timing of the hop. There should be four actions within the hop: a knee bend, a push-off (press against the floor), a lift off the floor, and a bent-knee landing on the same foot. To help students coincide their landing on the "a" cue, you might add a ready cue by saying "and-a, 1-and-2."
- Use a very slow count in order to give students time to learn all the extra footwork actions.

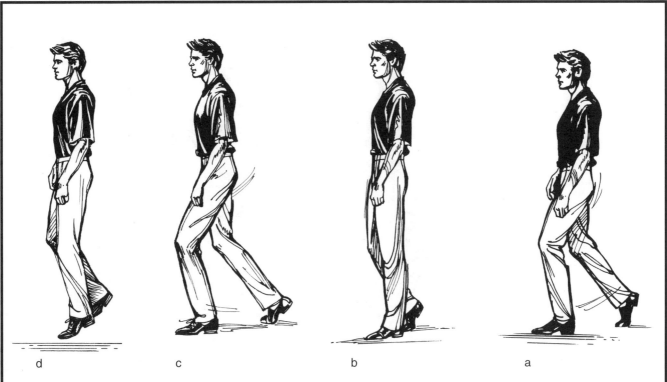

Figure 2.15   To decrease difficulty, start with the triple step (a-c), and then add the hop (d).

- If students have difficulty starting with the hop, ask them to start with the triple (see Figure 2.15a-c) (leave the hop out *only* when they take their first polka basic). Adding the hop at the end of the triple step is a more natural transition (see Figure 2.15d).
- Ask students to stand beside a partner without touching in order to get a feel for moving in relationship to a partner (you may provide scarves or other objects that partners could choose to hold instead of holding hands).
- Leave out the hop and only do consecutive triple steps.

To Increase Difficulty

- Focus students' attention on moving in unison with their partner, so that both outside feet, then both inside feet match as they execute the basic step.
- Encourage students to let their inside hands swing freely during the polka basics. With the outside foot, the upper torso slightly twists to let the inside arms swing back, then the outside elbows move forward (slightly facing the partner). With the inside foot, the upper torso slightly twists to let the inside arms swing forward, then the outside elbows move backward (with back slightly toward partner). These torso twists only need to be 45 degrees (see Figure 2.16, a and b).
- Without a partner, students may practice the basic polka step following different floor paths as follows: four polka basics forward, then four polka basics to make a 180-degree CW rotation (tracing a circular floor path), four polka basics forward, then four polka basics to make a 180-degree CCW rotation. This extension gives students new directions to move in and provides preliminary experiences with turns.

Figure 2.16 To increase difficulty, angle the shoulders 45 degrees (a) towards, then (b) away from partner to facilitate a natural swinging motion with the inside-joined hands.

2. *Polka Basic From a Semiopen Position*

Purpose and Organization

- The purpose of this drill is to introduce the semiopen position.
- Set up to travel in LOD.

Instructions to Class

- "Your basic polka step may also be executed from a semiopen position. Make sure that your extended hands do not pump; rather, the leader needs to keep the left arm firm and horizontal. Curve your extended elbows, and rotate your arms until the tip of your elbow points slightly to the side instead of down toward the floor. Look in the LOD."

Student Success Goal

- Competently demonstrate the basic step with a partner in a semiopen position, to counts, and to music.

To Decrease Difficulty

- Use very slow counts.
- Work in unison with your partner to alternately match both outside (away from partner) feet, then both inside (closest to partner) feet.

To Increase Difficulty

- Travel in LOD.

3. *Transition From an Inside-Hands Joined To a Semiopen Position*

Purpose and Organization

- This drill shows students how to connect two partner positions: from an inside-hands joined position to a semiopen position, then back to an inside-hands joined position—to create a continuous cycle of movements.
- Set up to travel in LOD.

Instructions to Class

- "At first, group together three sets of four

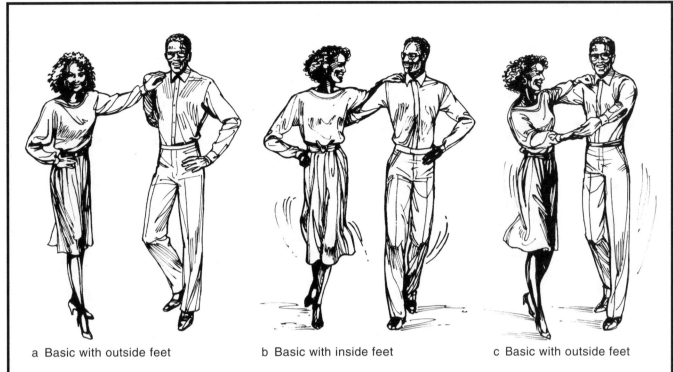

a Basic with outside feet   b Basic with inside feet   c Basic with outside feet

Figure 2.17 Transition leads from an inside-hands joined position to a semiopen position.

polka basics (eight counts per set) during each part of the transition from one partner position to another."

From an Inside-Hands Joined Position

Figure 2.17 shows the transition leads from an inside-hands joined position to a semiopen position.

- "Do two polka basics, letting the inside arms swing freely (backward, then forward)."
- "On the third polka basic (with outside foot), the leader rotates his upper torso approximately 45 degrees in order to face his partner. This rotation lets the inside arms swing higher, so that the leader can place the follower's hand on his right shoulder (see Figure 2.17a)."
- "During the fourth polka basic (with inside foot), the leader releases the follower's hand, places his hand just below her left shoulder blade (see Figure 2.17b), and extends his left hand forward for the follower to place her hand in his (see Figure 2.17c)."
- "Do four polka basics in semiopen position."

From a Semiopen Position

Figure 2.18 shows the transition leads from a semiopen position to an inside-hands joined position.

- "On the first polka basic, the leader gently pushes his partner away (see Figure 2.18a). On the second polka basic, both partners slide down arms to grasp hands (back to an inside-hands joined position) (see Figure 2.18b)."
- "On the third and fourth polka basics, let the inside arms swing freely (backward [see Figure 2.18c], then forward)."

Student Success Goal

- Competently demonstrate the transition from an inside-hands joined position to a semiopen position, then back to an inside-hands joined position, to music.

To Decrease Difficulty

- Have students do only the arm motions with no footwork until they feel the flow and can smoothly transition from one partner position to the next.
- Isolate each part, gradually adding another as it is mastered.

To Increase Difficulty

- Challenge students to use three sets of two polka basics when executing these transitions.

a Basic with outside feet   b Basic with inside feet   c Basic with outside feet

Figure 2.18 Transition leads from a semiopen position to an inside-hands joined position.

4. *Polka Basic From a Closed Position*

Purpose and Organization

- This drill introduces the closed position.
- Set up to travel in LOD.

Instructions to Class

- "From a closed-partner position, the followers travel backward while the leaders travel forward. Make sure that your feet move in unison with your partner, on the same side. Take small steps. Followers need to reach from their hip (instead of bending their knees) when traveling backward and to contact the floor in a toe-ball-heel motion. Check your starting position to make sure that your feet are not toe-to-toe with your partner's; rather, they should be offset (one-half step to your own left side, with one foot in-between your partner's feet)."

Student Success Goal

- Competently demonstrate the basic step with a partner in a closed position, to counts, and to music.

To Decrease Difficulty

- Start from a modified partner position by gently touching fingertips with the partner.
- Use a very slow tempo.

To Increase Difficulty

- Increase the tempo.

5. *Transition From a Closed to a Semiopen Position*

Purpose and Organization

- The purpose of this drill is to move from a closed position to a semiopen position, then back to a closed position again, creating a continuous, closed-loop cycle. Two sets of four polka basics are used, then a set of two polka basics.
- Set up to travel in the LOD.

Instructions to Class

From a Closed Position

- "At the end of any even-numbered basic (start with four basics), the leader gently presses the heel of his right hand on the follower's left shoulder blade as he rotates his upper torso CW 90 degrees to point his left hand toward the LOD. The follower pivots on the ball of her left foot to make a CW half turn to face the LOD. These actions bring the follower to the leader's right side, into a semiopen position."

From a Semiopen Position

- "Do four polka basics in semiopen position. Your upper torso should be facing 45 degrees toward your partner, while your lower body and feet still point toward the LOD."
- "The transition to return to closed position takes two polka basics. On the first polka basic, the leader rotates his upper torso CCW 90 degrees, which brings the follower CCW a half turn to face the man. Both partners do the second polka basic in closed position."

Student Success Goal

- Competently demonstrate the transition from a closed position to a semiopen position, then back to a closed position, to counts, and to music.

To Decrease Difficulty

- Isolate each set, then combine in an accumulative manner.

To Increase Difficulty

- Reduce the number of polka basics in each set to two.
- Connect any three partner positions. For example, start in an inside-hands joined position, move to semiopen position, and move to closed position. Or, start in a semiopen position, move to closed, and move to semiopen position again.

Introducing Fox-Trot and Waltz Basics

Because the fox-trot box variations are identical to those used in the waltz, you may introduce them together. Both the fox-trot and the waltz basics are executed in the LOD. This section introduces students to the fox-trot and waltz basics with a partner in closed position. The box rhythm variations for both fox-trot and waltz include a box step, a left-box turn, and half-box progressions forward (and backward). The magic rhythm variation only in fox-trot is the magic step. Additional variation options and partner positions will be covered in Step 6 (for the fox-trot) and in Step 7 (for the waltz).

The fox-trot is an American dance first introduced in 1913 or 1914 by a musical comedy star, Mr. Harry Fox, who performed a fast, trotting step to ragtime music in a Ziegfeld musical. Because this early version was too exhausting, it was modified a number of times into a smooth, graceful dance characterized by erect posture and stationary torso and arms (frame). There are two rhythm options within the fox-trot: Westchester box rhythm and magic rhythm. The box rhythm is a four-count combination of one slow and two quicks. Arthur Murray created the magic step, which uses the magic rhythm, a six-count combination of two slows and two quicks. These basic fox-trot rhythms may be intermixed within practice sequences for more variety.

The waltz is a smooth dance that became popular after two Austrian composers, Johann Strauss and Franz Lanner, created beautiful waltz music in the 1800s. The waltz is char-acterized by erect posture, stationary torso and arms (frame), and a gentle, wavelike rise-and-fall motion.

Your students will soon notice that the fox-trot box variations are identical to the waltz variations with one major difference: The former uses uneven rhythm (i.e., three weight changes within four beats), while the latter uses even rhythm (i.e., one weight change per beat). Review the note values on page 26.

EXECUTION AND STYLING

The fox-trot is done to 4/4-time music, with four beats per measure (each getting one count), while the waltz is done to 3/4-time music, with three beats per measure (each getting one count). For ease of learning, this book highlights the footwork strategy of matching an action with each beat when teaching the fox-trot box step variations. Thus, the students are given *footwork actions* that correspond to each beat (i.e., are treated as an even rhythm), while the *rhythm* (with the music) is slow, quick, quick (uneven). The extra, non-weight bearing action on Count 2 is also a styling move that accentuates the more jazzy, swinglike music played for the fox-trot.

Be prepared to recognize and modify your instructions to fit at least two student skill levels: beginning and accomplished. Note that the beginning student responses reflect typical errors while the accomplished student responses reflect the desired execution and styling. Use the technique and styling criteria in the following rating chart in either an informal or a formal way to assess proper execution and styling of the basic box rhythm (fox-trot and waltz) as well as the magic rhythm (fox-trot).

Box and Magic Rhythm Technique and Styling Rating Chart

CRITERION	BEGINNING	ACCOMPLISHED
Closed Position	• Elbows are close to body (with space in-between his right and her left arms) • Stand toe-to-toe with partner	• Elbows are curved and lifted (his right and her left arms lightly touch) • Stand offset (she is one-half step to his right, so that his right foot is in-between her feet)
Box Rhythm Execution 　a. **During "slow"**	• Short reach • Ball of foot slides on floor • Toes angle out with a wide base	• Long reach • Weight transfers heel-to-ball • Feet parallel within a narrow base
b. **During "quick"**	• Wide side step	• Shoulder-width (or smaller) side step
c. **During "quick"**	• Weight change with feet apart	• Weight change with feet together (close)
Magic Rhythm Execution (Fox-trot only) 　a. **During "slow, slow"**	• Two short reaches • Ball of foot slides on floor	• Two long reaches • Weight transfers heel-to-ball
b. **During "quick, quick"**	• Same as box rhythm	• Same as box rhythm
Styling 　a. **Waltz**	• Square box shape on floor • Head height remains level • Free leg swings inward toward other leg prior to side step, then close	• Rectangular box shape on floor • Gentle rise and fall (low, high, medium level) • Free leg cuts diagonally to side step, then close
b. **Fox-trot**	• Free leg cuts diagonally to side step, then close	• Free leg swings from hip, tracing a 90-degree angle on floor, prior to side step, then close

Drills for Short Fox-Trot and Waltz Combinations

1. Basic Techniques in Closed Position

Purpose and Organization

- The purpose of this drill is to introduce students to the basic footwork and styling for the waltz and the fox-trot within a closed-dance position. The direction of movement is stationary for the box step (both waltz and fox-trot) and LOD for the magic step (fox-trot only).
- Both parts are identical for the box step and may be taught at the same time. When to start differs as the leaders start on the forward half (with left foot), and the followers start on the backward half (with right foot).

Instructions to Class

- "The only difference between the fox-trot box step and the waltz box step is the rhythm. Both use the same 'slow, quick, quick' (or box rhythm), yet the number of counts are different because the fox-trot box step gets four beats per measure while the waltz box step gets three beats per measure. In addition, the fox-trot magic step uses a magic rhythm, or 'slow,

slow, quick, quick,' that gets six beats (within 1-1/2 measures). The timing of the 'slow' versus the 'quick' is relative, and represents approximately a 2:1 ratio."
- "Both the leader's and the follower's parts are identical and only vary according to which half is executed first (the leader starts with the forward half, and the follower starts with the backward half."

Box Step (Waltz)

Figure 2.19 shows the waltz box-step footwork.

- *Footwork:* Three weight changes, repeated on both sides of the body.
- *Rhythmic pattern:* SSS, SSS
- *Counts:* **1**, 2, 3, **4**, 5, 6 (both sides of the body); or, **1**, 2, 3; **2**, 2, 3; . . . (eight basics comprise a phrase of music)
- *Styling:* Lengthen the stride on Count 1 in order to make the step length better match the accented first count (downbeat) of the music. The free foot cuts di-

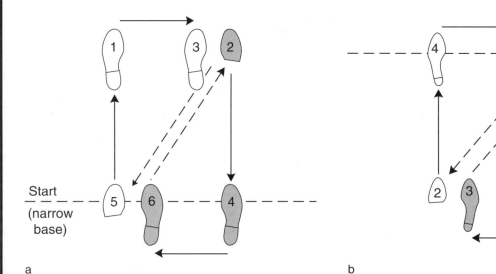

a   b

Figure 2.19   Waltz box-step footwork (a) for the leader, and (b) for the follower.

Box Step (Fox-Trot)

Figure 2.20 shows the fox-trot box-step footwork.

- *Footwork:* Three weight changes, repeated on both sides of the body
- *Rhythmic pattern:* SQQ; SQQ
- *Counts:* 1-2, 3, 4, 5-6, 7, 8 (both sides of the body); or, **1-2**, 3, 4; **2-2**, 3, 4; . . . (eight basics within a phrase of music)
- *Styling:* Notice that there are no weight changes on Counts 2 and 6. In this book, on Count 2, a nonweight action has been purposely added to contrast the styling differences within the waltz and the fox-trot box steps, that is, prior to the side step, the free leg swings from the hip with foot flexed at the ankle, to trace a 90-degree angle on the floor and briefly bring feet together (without a weight change). This nonweight action gives students something to do to account for the extra time (two counts of music) during the "slow." Or, students may wait to transfer weight on Count 2 (at the end of the "slow").

Magic Step (Fox-Trot)

Figure 2.21 shows the magic-step footwork.

- *Footwork:* Four weight changes
- *Rhythmic pattern:* SSQQ

agonally to the side—there is no time to bring the feet together briefly (without a weight change), as may be done in the fox-trot styling.

- *Counts:* 1-2, 3-4, 5, 6
- *Styling:* Strive for long, reaching steps on the slows and short, sideward steps on the quicks. As a styling option on Count 4, let the ball of the free foot briefly touch the instep of the other foot, then continue directly to the side on Count 5 (making a sharp, 90-degree angle).
- "The leader needs to transfer body weight forward onto the ball of each foot to signal forward motion. If light elbow contact is made with partner, then the follower should be able to feel this slight upper torso movement and begin to move backward. If there is a hesitation in forward momentum, then the leader signals a reduction in forward motion. The leader needs to assertively continue forward for two walking steps instead of only one walking step, then take regular side, close steps."

Student Success Goal

- Competently demonstrate each of the three basic steps (waltz box step, fox-trot box step, and fox-trot magic step) alone, to counts, to music, then with a partner in a closed position, to counts, and to music.

To Decrease Difficulty

- Have leaders stand with back and heels against a wall. Ask them to take a step or two away from the wall and to notice which part of their body leaves the wall first. (It will be the upper torso, which is

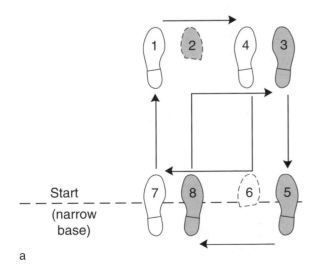

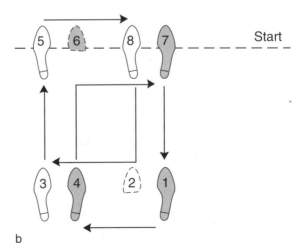

Figure 2.20   Fox-trot box-step footwork (a) for the leader, and (b) for the follower.

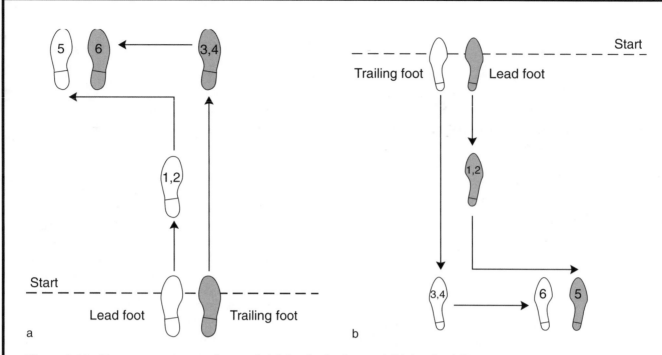

Figure 2.21   Fox-trot magic-step footwork (a) for the leader, and (b) for the follower.

the leader's nonverbal lead to signal forward motion.)
- Use a modified partner position with partners gently touching fingertips in order to help each partner define his or her own space (avoid collapsing elbows to let one partner invade the other's space).

To Increase Difficulty
- Ask the followers to close their eyes and kinesthetically feel the leader's leads.
- In the fox-trot, combine both rhythms within a set routine; alternately complete two boxes in place, then two magic steps forward.

2. *Left Box-Turn*

Purpose and Organization
- This drill shows students how to rotate CCW using two box steps to complete a 360-degree turn with a partner. Students have been moving forward and backward. Now, they will need to be aware of two additional directions: the forward, left diagonal, and the backward, right diagonal. These directions represent intermediate points in-between the original front wall and the next CCW wall they will face.
- Because students will be making a 90-degree turn on each half box step, you can orient them to face a new wall each time. When moving in the LOD, the students will be facing center of circle, reverse LOD, outside of circle, and LOD (at the end of each half box).

- The left-box turn leads are the same for both the waltz and the fox-trot. However, the timing of when to use these leads differs.

Figures 2.22 and 2.23 show the left-box turn footwork for the waltz and the fox-trot, respectively.

Instructions to Class
- Start in a closed position. It is easier to lead a turn after executing the box step (once the tempo and unison with your partner is established). At the end of a box step, the leader rotates his upper torso and arms 45-degrees CCW, which places his shoulders perpendicular to his left front diagonal direction. This upper body rotation facilitates either a toe-out or a toe-in position, depending upon

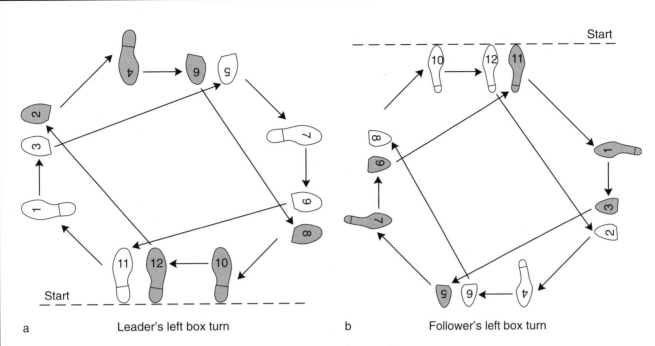

Figure 2.22 Left-box turn footwork for the waltz (12 total counts).

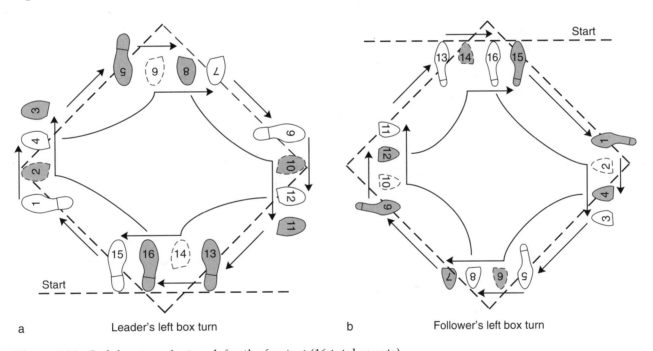

Figure 2.23 Left-box turn footwork for the fox-trot (16 total counts).

whether you are on the forward half (leaders start here) or the backward half (followers start here)."

• "On the 'quick, quick' counts, continue rotating another 45-degrees to face a new wall (and complete a 90-degree turn). Repeat these actions (alternating your toe position) to face all four walls. Remember that the body goes where the shoul-

ders go, so continue rotating from the waist to continue the turn."

• "To signal that the turn is over, the leader firmly maintains frame (with arms in closed dance position) while facing the LOD and transfers his weight forward to signal the next basic (box step or magic step)."

Student Success Goal

- Competently demonstrate a left-box turn (in waltz, then in fox-trot timing) alone, to counts, to music, then with a partner in a closed position, to counts, and to music.

To Decrease Difficulty

- Ask students to practice the upper torso rotation by twisting from the waist and keeping the arms connected to the shoulders.
- Freeze students' positions on the first

"slow" in order to check their foot position (either left toe is angled out, on forward half, or right toe is angled in, on backward half) and their shoulder position (angled 45 degrees, in-between front wall and next wall).

To Increase Difficulty

- Alternate two boxes (in place) with a left-box turn.
- *Fox-trot only:* Start with a box step, then alternate at least one left-box turn with at least two magic steps.

3. Half-Box Progressions

Purpose and Organization

- This drill uses a half box in the forward direction to progress in the LOD. A backward direction is also introduced for practice with the leader facing the LOD and traveling in reverse LOD.
- In Step 6 (fox-trot) and Step 7 (waltz), a transition will be introduced to let the leader progress in the LOD while execut-

ing backward half-box progressions. Thus, students need to know that the backward direction presented here is for practice only, and it is not a viable option when the LOD is open on the dance floor until it is modified to progress in the LOD.

- Set up in closed position, with the leaders all facing the same wall. Be careful

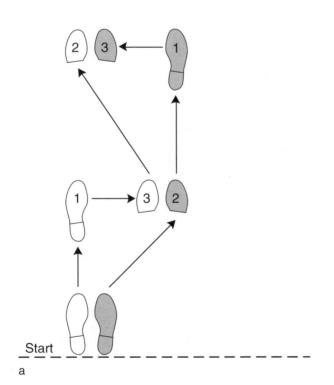
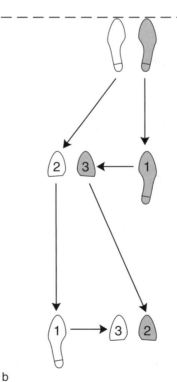

a   b

Figure 2.24 Waltz half-box progressions forward (a) for the leader, and (b) for the follower.

that the backward direction is clear of obstacles and other couples.

- As a general rule, keep repetitions in multiples of two so that the leader will always be leading into a new step with his left foot. Another way of stating this is to tell students to do two rhythmic patterns of "slow, quick, quick" before changing to another variation.

- Beginning students need more time to prepare for the next lead, so this drill repeats the half-box progression four times.

Figures 2.24 and 2.25 show the half-box progression-forward footwork for the waltz and the fox-trot, respectively.

Instructions to Class

- "Within the box step, you executed a half-box forward, then a half-box backward. In half-box progressions, the half boxes are executed in the same direction (either forward or backward). The cues for the half-box progressions forward are 'forward, side, close; forward, side, close.' "

- "At the end of the first half box and prior to the next half box, the leader must continue to transfer body weight forward onto the ball of each working foot. This cues the follower to continue moving in the same direction, only reaching with the other foot to do another half-box progression. If the leader hesitates even slightly in-between each half box progression, then the follower will think that the leader wants to do a box step. So, the leaders need to be assertive, and initiate forward motion leads before the next basic begins."

- "For practice with the backward half-box progressions, alternate four half-box progressions forward, then four half-box progressions backward. The lead occurs at the end of the fourth half-box progression forward by keeping the leader's right hand very firm on the follower's left shoulder blade and gently pulling his hand toward his midline. This action signals the follower to reverse directions. At the end of the four half-box progressions backward, the leader does his nor-

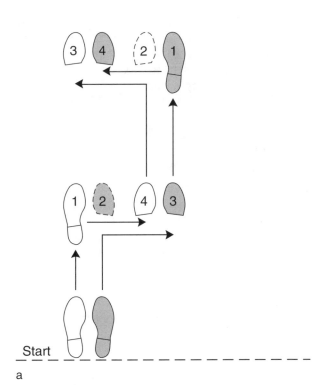

a

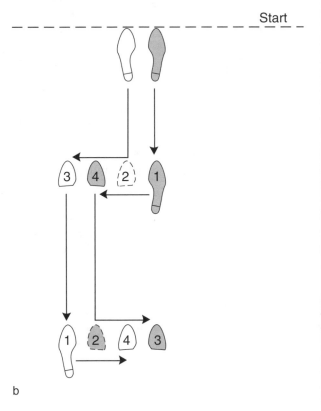

b

Figure 2.25   Fox-trot half-box progressions forward (a) for the leader, and (b) for the follower.

mal weight transfer forward to signal forward direction. This option may be desired on a very crowded floor where the only direction open is backward—be sure to look first. It should not be used on a dance floor with a designated LOD."

Student Success Goal

- Competently demonstrate half-box progressions (forward and backward in waltz, then in fox-trot timing) alone, to counts, to music, then with a partner in closed position, to counts, and to music.

To Decrease Difficulty

- Start with at least two box steps before leading half-box progressions forward.

- Use a modified partner position, such as fingertip pressure with partner, to signal direction.

To Increase Difficulty

- Alternate two left-box turns with four half-box progressions.
- Let students combine any two or three basics, for example, do two quarter turns left (one half of a left-box turn), do four half-box progressions backward, then do two quarter turns left (remaining half of a left-box turn). This combination has the advance of traveling in the LOD (until students know the fancier transition covered later in Steps 6 and 7).

4. Combine Four Leads

Purpose and Organization

- This drill helps students identify the decision-making options that the leader has when combining at least four different leads to create a short sequence.
- Partners in closed position, with the leaders all facing the LOD.

Instructions to Class

- "You know how to do four basics using box rhythm: the box step, half-box progressions forward, half-box progressions backward, and a left-box turn. You also know how to do one basic using magic rhythm: the magic step within the fox-trot."
- "Experiment with the most effective ways to combine these basics in order to create a cluster of moves (or short sequence). You may alternately repeat any four of these basics as long as you do any even-numbered repetitions of each."

Student Success Goal

- Competently demonstrate at least four different short sequences that combine at least four different leads.

To Decrease Difficulty

- Gradually combine any two basics that progress in the LOD. One suggestion for

helping students learn how to turn at the corners of the room is to combine half-box progressions forward for the length of the room, do one quarter-turn (first portion of a left-box turn), and immediately go into half-box progressions forward (with leader's right foot). Or, the leader can very gradually rotate his upper torso, like turning a car wheel, and do continuous half-box progressions in the LOD along a curved path.

- Combine any three box-rhythm basics (whether or not traveling in the LOD).
- Provide students with specific suggestions for solving the drill's Success Goal, such as the following:

a. Four boxes in place, two left-box turns, two boxes, and a left-box turn (*Note:* This is an example of decelerated rhythm because the numbers decrease by half [4, 2, 1]. If the reverse occurs, it is an example of accelerated rhythm, which is more difficult.)

b. Two boxes in place, a left-box turn, four half-box progressions forward, two left-box turns

c. Four boxes in place, six half-box progressions forward, two left quarter turns, four half-box progressions backward, two left quarter turns

To Increase Difficulty

- Repeat entire sequence for the length of a song.
- Use the minimum number of repetitions for each basic, such as one box in place, two half-box progressions forward, a left-box turn, two half-box progressions forward.
- *In fox-trot only:* Encourage students to mix box and magic rhythms, as follows:

  a. Four boxes in place, either half-box progressions forward, two left-box turns, six magic steps

  b. Two boxes in place, four magic steps, four half-box progressions forward, two magic steps

- Ask students to create spontaneous sequences involving basics known so far.

Summary

As your students learn the basic steps in at least one partner position, encourage them to demonstrate proper etiquette both to their partners, by saying "thank you" and by not criticizing each other, and to other couples, by modifying their sequences to fit the floor traffic. As a review for all basics, you might play Side B of the soundsheet (located in *Social Dance*), which plays 90 seconds of music for each basic covered in this book, or pre-tape a variety of your own selections. Let students decide for themselves which basic best fits the music played. This would also be a good time to rate technique execution, whether by yourself or by student partners. You might consider reviewing the basics in a novel way (to test students' abilities to transfer knowledge to new situations) by introducing some of the mixers presented in Step 8 of this book. Mixers are fun ways to develop a sense of group unity and cooperation.

Step 3 Adding Swing Variations for Longer Combinations

At this point, students should know how to execute the swing basics when in two partner positions (a semiopen position and a one-hand joined position) and to demonstrate two transitions (an arch-out/arch-in and a roll-out/roll-in), creating a short sequence starting in a semiopen position, moving to a one-hand joined position, then coming back to a semiopen position. Assign appropriate drills from Step 2, if your students do not have these prerequisite skills, or if you want to review these skills.

By the end of this instructor step, your students should be able to

- execute the basics when in a two-hands joined position;
- demonstrate two additional transitions (a half-rotation transition and a release of one hand during an unwrap) to move from a one-hand joined position to a two-hands joined position, then back to a one-hand joined position;
- execute at least two variations when in each of three different partner positions (combining at least four to six leads); and
- create spontaneous sequences that connect all three partner positions while demonstrating proper floor and partner etiquette.

PRACTICE PROCEDURES TO FACILITATE DECISION MAKING

During early learning stages, it is helpful for students to follow a set routine that is provided for them. After memorizing it, they will often ask, "What do I do next?" This response is your cue that these students are ready to take on more decision making in order to create their own sequences. The swing drills in this step are organized according to the dance position in which they are executed and gradually build in more student choices. The practice procedures move from a closed situation (keeping the same tempo, sequence

order, and amount of space) to an open situation (varying the tempo, sequence order, and amount of space). Use a whole-part-whole approach to present variations, and point out appropriate comparisons and contrasts. When students have difficulty, follow the general procedures presented in Step 2. Position the leaders to face the same direction. As students become more accomplished decision makers, they will be able to increase the number of skills combined in any one sequence. They will also be able to modify their sequences to best fit the floor density (establishing their own spot without bumping into others) and to complement their partners (dancing in unison with a partner instead of one partner deliberately overshadowing the other, or the leader throwing his partner around).

SWING COMBINATION OPTIONS

Chart 3.1 summarizes the swing variation and transition options covered in this book and shows the interrelationship among the three dance positions (making two closed-loop cycles). The variation and transition options are appropriate for all three swing tempos and are grouped according to the dance position from which they are executed. You may teach selected variations or options when in each position. For example, the leader has three choices when in a semiopen position: (1) execute the basic step in-place, (2) rotate CW while executing the basic step, or (3) rotate CCW while executing the basic step. In addition, the options increase because the leader may lead these variations in any order, using any number of repetitions, and adding any number of basic steps in-between. The drills gradually connect two positions (with more variation options), then three positions—to create longer practice combinations and to provide guidelines for creating spontaneous sequences on the dance floor.

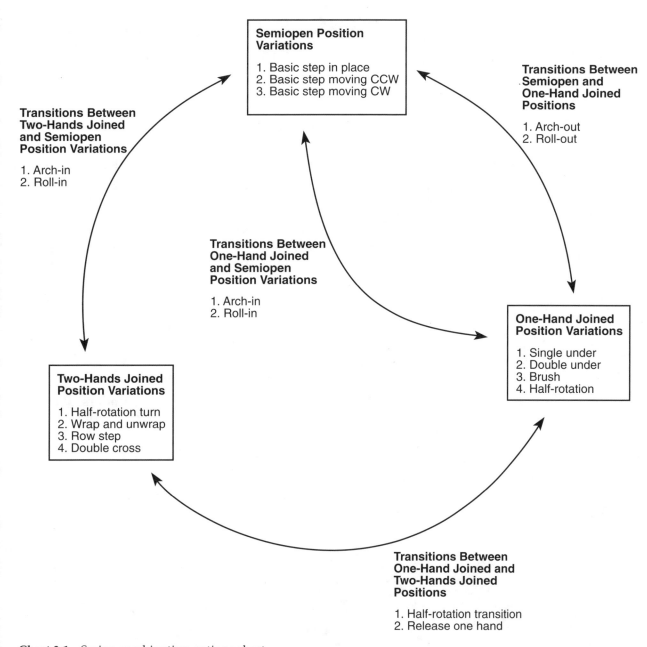

Semiopen Position Variations

1. Basic step in place
2. Basic step moving CCW
3. Basic step moving CW

Transitions Between Semiopen and One-Hand Joined Positions

1. Arch-out
2. Roll-out

Transitions Between Two-Hands Joined and Semiopen Position Variations

1. Arch-in
2. Roll-in

Transitions Between One-Hand Joined and Semiopen Position Variations

1. Arch-in
2. Roll-in

One-Hand Joined Position Variations

1. Single under
2. Double under
3. Brush
4. Half-rotation

Two-Hands Joined Position Variations

1. Half-rotation turn
2. Wrap and unwrap
3. Row step
4. Double cross

Transitions Between One-Hand Joined and Two-Hands Joined Positions

1. Half-rotation transition
2. Release one hand

Chart 3.1   Swing combination options chart.

STUDENT KEYS TO SUCCESS

Watch for the following execution techniques in each drill.

- Keep elbows slightly bent in order to stay close to your partner and maintain posture.

- Lightly maintain fingertip pressure with partner during turns.
- Fluidly execute basics within combinations.
- Use appropriate styling.
- Leads should rotate both partners within their own spot.

Drills for Swing Variations: From a One-Hand Joined Position

1. Single Under

Purpose and Organization

- This drill introduces movement for the leader such that both partners switch places (making a 180-degree exchange of places).
- Set up in rows of partners in a one-hand joined position with the leaders all facing the same direction.

Instructions to Class

- "The initial lead for the single under during the ball, change is the same as for the arch-in transition that you already learned (see Figure 3.1a), with one exception. Now, the leader exchanges positions with his partner, in a 180-degree switch, by spinning CW on the ball of his left foot on Count 2—at the end of the first 'slow' (see Figure 3.1b)."
- "Both partners face each other on the second 'slow,' ready for the ball, change (see Figure 3.1c). At this time the leader has two options: (1) repeat the single under lead by pulling his left hand toward his right shoulder, or (2) lead the arch-in transition back to a semiopen position. If he chooses the former, he needs to continue exchanging places with his partner. If he chooses the latter, then he moves to his left (to be on the left side of the triangle) in order to give the follower room to move to his right side, and he places his right palm on her left shoulder blade. Experiment with both options, using any number of single unders."

Student Success Goal

- Two consecutive single unders, then an arch-in transition, with a partner, to swing music.

To Decrease Difficulty

- Do each option separately.
- Combine one single under and an arch-in.

a Ball, change   b Slow   c Slow

Figure 3.1   Single under.

- Add basics to give more decision-making time.

To Increase Difficulty

- Start in a semiopen position, do an arch-out transition, one or more single unders, then an arch-in transition (to create a three-lead sequence that both starts and ends in the semiopen position).

2. Double Under

Purpose and Organization

- This drill adds a delayed underarm turn for the leader, who turns immediately after the follower's underarm turn (see Figure 3.2).
- Set up in rows of partners in a one-hand joined position, with the leaders facing the same direction.

Instructions to Class

- "The follower's part in the double under is the same as in the single under. However, now the leader also gets to turn. To avoid hitting heads in the middle, the leader must make sure that the follower's turn is completed *before* he turns CCW under his left arm (on the second 'slow'). You should end up reversing positions 180 degrees and facing each other for the ball-change steps. The lead for the next variation occurs during the ball, change. If no lead is given, do the basic step in place."
- "Now the leader has three variation choices: single under, double under, or arch-in. Experiment with each option, using any number of repetitions of the single under and of the double under."

Student Success Goal

- Correctly execute each of the 3 options after a double under, with a partner, to music.

To Decrease Difficulty

- Do each option separately.
- Combine any two options.

To Increase Difficulty

- Increase the length of the sequence by

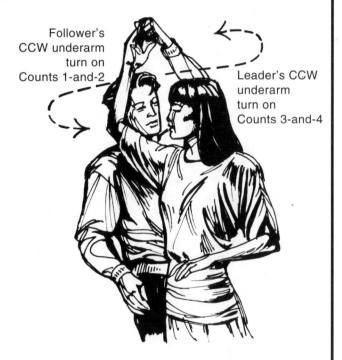

Follower's CCW underarm turn on Counts 1-and-2

Leader's CCW underarm turn on Counts 3-and-4

Figure 3.2   Double under.

starting from a semiopen position, executing in-place basics, rotations either CW or CCW, and arch-out into the one-hand joined position. Then add any number of repetitions of the single under and of the double under, then lead an arch-in (back to a semiopen position).
- Vary the order (e.g., try the double under prior to the single under).
- Vary the transition used (yielding four more choices: either matching arch-out and arch-in, roll-out and roll-in, or mixing transitions, using, for example, an arch-out and a roll-in).

3. Half-Rotation Turn

Purpose and Organization

- Another way to exchange positions with a partner is to do a half-rotation turn.
- Set up with partners in a one-hand joined position, with the leaders all facing the same direction.

Instructions to Class

- "Another variation from a one-hand joined position is a half-rotation turn. The lead is very similar to the roll-in transition back into the semiopen position, except that the leader now turns as well (like he did in the single under) and keeps a one-hand joined position. The half-rotation turn permits rotation while doing the basic step."
- "Both prior to and on the first 'slow,' the leader holds his left hand approximately waist high and traces a horizontal "J" in the air (see Figure 3.3a). Both partners spin 180-degrees CW on the ball of their foot (the leader's left and the follower's right) and face at the second 'slow' (see Figure 3.3b). Partners remain facing to

do the ball-change ('quick, quick'). Be careful that you don't get too far away from your partner and that you use small steps."
- "Experiment with alternating either the single under or the double under with the half-rotation turn. Notice that the leads alternately move from a vertical to a horizontal plane."

Student Success Goal

- Demonstrate a fluid sequence that alternates either the single or double under with the half-rotation turn, with a partner, to music.

To Decrease Difficulty

- Add a basic after each half-rotation turn.

To Increase Difficulty

- Combine these three variations in any order.
- Start from a semiopen position and combine at least five leads that include a transition to a one-hand joined position, then back to a semiopen position.

a Initiate "J" stroke after ball, change

b Exchange positions on second slow

Figure 3.3   Half-rotation turn.

4. Brush

Purpose and Organization

- A variation of the half-rotation turn is a brush step. This variation lets the leader do a fancy turn.
- Set up in rows of partners in a one-hand joined position, with the leaders all facing the same direction.

Instructions to Class

- "As you do a basic in-place, the leader transfers the follower's right hand from his left hand into his right hand during the second 'slow.'"
- "During the first 'slow' of the next basic, the leader passes right shoulders with his partner as he rotates his right wrist CCW (as if turning a door knob), keeping his hand below his waist (see Figure 3.4a)."
- "During the second 'slow,' the leader turns CCW and passes the follower's hand back into his left hand, still keeping the pass at hip level in order to avoid hitting the follower with any bent elbows. The follower does her regular CW half-rotation turn (see Figure 3.4b)."
- "Face each other during the 'quick, quick' counts (see Figure 3.4c). At the end of the brush, the leader will find that his left hand is in an unusual grasp. To return to the normal swing grasp, lead one of two options: a single under or a double under."

Student Success Goal

- Demonstrate a fluid sequence that alternates a brush step with either a single under or a double under while in a one-hand joined position, to music.

To Decrease Difficulty

- Add a basic step in place before the brush step (swivel on the balls of the feet in order to keep the steps small).
- Lead any number of repetitions of the single or double under after the brush.

To Increase Difficulty

- Require both a single under and a double under (in random order) after the brush step.
- Set up for the brush during a single under, with the leader transferring the follower's right hand from his left to his right on the second "slow" of the single under (increasing his timing). Then do the brush step on the next swing basic.
- Practice at least six leads together to create a long sequence that both starts and ends with a semiopen position. Initially, use the following order: arch-out, half-rotation turn, single under, brush step, double under, and arch-in.
- Vary the order, the number of repetitions, and the length.

a Brush right shoulders to lead   b Follower turns CW; leader turns CCW   c Ball, change

Figure 3.4 Brush step.

Drills for Swing Variations: From a Two-Hands Joined Position

5. *Transition to the Two-Hands Joined Position*

Purpose and Organization

- This drill introduces one way to get from a one-hand joined position to a two-hands joined position.
- Set up in rows of partners in a one-hand joined position, with the leaders all facing the same direction.

Instructions to Class

- "An easy way to get into a two-hands joined position with your partner is to modify the half-turn rotation that you already know. The goal is to camouflage the grasping of the second hand. On the first 'slow,' the leader traces a horizontal 'J' stroke with his left hand and cups his right hand, placing it palm up and close to the outside of his right hip (see Figure 3.5). The momentum of the half-rotation turn brings both partners closer together so that the follower merely places her left hand in his palm. The leader may do any number of repetitions of the half-rotation turn while in the two-hands joined position."
- "One way to get back to a one-hand joined position is to lead a single under and to release the leader's right hand grasp."

Student Success Goal

- Demonstrate a fluid transition from a one-hand joined position into a two-hands joined position, then back to a one-hand joined position, to music.

To Decrease Difficulty

- Do more repetitions of the half-turn rotation before leading into a two-hands joined position.

To Increase Difficulty

- As another option to get back to a one-hand joined position, the leader can lead a double under and release one hand.

Figure 3.5   Present hand and transition to a two-hands joined position when bodies come closer on the turn.

6. *Wrap and Unwrap*

Purpose and Organization

- Another variation option when in a two-hands joined position is a wrap and unwrap.
- Set up in rows of partners in a two-hands joined position, with the leaders all facing the same direction.

Instructions to Class

- "To initiate the wrap from a two-hands joined position, the leader must bring both hands across his midline to his right side while maintaining his location (instead of exchanging places with his partner). He has two simultaneous leads: to bring his right hand low and to his right side, and to lift his left hand high and CCW above the follower's head (see Figure 3.6a). The follower's part is exactly the same as for a single under, except the leader will not release his hand grasps, and she will end up on his right side. Both partners finish the second 'slow' and the ball-change while in this wrap position (see Figure 3.6b)."
- "To unwrap, the leader lifts his left arm to form an arch (see Figure 3.6c). Time this left-arm lift to be after the 'ball-change.' At the end of the first 'slow,' the leader gently presses with the heel of his right hand on his partner's back (to signal the turn on Count 2 under the arched arms). Both partners face each other to do the rest of the basic step. If these actions feel familiar, it is because they reverse the order of the arch-out and arch-in transition leads—now from a two-hands joined position."
- "When in the wrap position, do at least two basics before leading the unwrap. An easy way to get back to the one-hand joined position is for the leader to release his right hand during the unwrap."

a Slow   b Slow (to wrap)   c Ball, change (to unwrap)

Figure 3.6 Wrap and unwrap.

Student Success Goal

- Demonstrate fluid transitions both into and out of the wrap position, to music.

To Decrease Difficulty

- Do any number of basics while in the wrap or unwrap positions.
- Stay in a two-hands joined position.

To Increase Difficulty

- Do only one basic into, then one basic out of the wrap position.
- Start in a one-hand joined position, move to a two-hands joined position, then execute a wrap and an unwrap.

- Create a sequence that moves from a one-hand joined position to a two-hands joined position (include a wrap and an unwrap), then back to a one-hand joined position.
- Both partners may rotate in a CW direction during the wrap, if the leader moves forward to meet his partner.
- Once both partners are rotating, the leader may gently pull his right hand and continue the rotation by substituting two walks for the ball, change. To stop this CW partner rotation, the leader merely slows down and does a regular ball-change.

7. Row Step

Purpose and Organization

- This is a fun, two-hands joined position variation that requires momentum.
- Use the cues "right shoulder, left shoulder, shoulders square" (to correspond to the slow, slow, and ball-change, respectively).
- Notice that students may rotate at least two different ways with this variation. If the leader brings his feet together, then the amount of rotation is limited. However, if the leader crosses his right foot behind his left foot during the second "slow," then the rotation continues CW. If students want to get almost 360 degrees of rotation on the row variation, then encourage the latter technique. It's also more fun!
- Set up in rows of partners in a two-hands joined position, with the leaders all facing the same direction.

Instructions to Class

- "The row step takes advantage of centrifugal force. Try the leads first, then add the footwork. Prior to the first 'slow,' the leader extends his right arm and brings his left elbow back, as if he is drawing an arrow in a bow. These actions bring his right shoulder closer to his partner's right shoulder (with shoulders on a 45-degree angle). Then, he re-

verses his arm pull on the second 'slow' by extending his left arm and bringing his right elbow back, again as if he is drawing an arrow in a bow. These actions bring his left shoulder closer to his partner's left shoulder (with shoulders on a 45-degree angle). On the 'quick, quick,' do your regular ball-change, facing your partner with shoulders parallel (or square to each other)."

- "After you feel comfortable with the arm leads, add the footwork. Because the row step involves rotating, it is easier to take only one step on each of the 'slows' (using a single-lindy basic, regardless of the tempo of the music). Imagine a small circle (approximately one foot in diameter) on the floor. On the first 'slow,' angle your foot (the leader's left foot and follower's right foot) to step forward and toward your left-diagonal front. Check that your foot is both within the circle and parallel with your partner's foot (see Figure 3.7a). Pivot on this foot to bring your left shoulders (and hips) closer together. To add more rotation, the leader crosses his right foot behind his left while the follower brings her feet together (see Figure 3.7b). Switching the arms increases the amount of rotation. Face each other to do the 'ball-change' steps (see Figure 3.7c)."

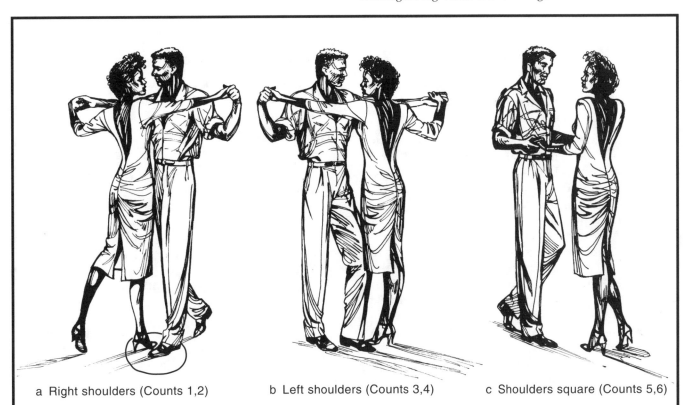

a Right shoulders (Counts 1,2)   b Left shoulders (Counts 3,4)   c Shoulders square (Counts 5,6)

Figure 3.7 Row step.

- "The row step is difficult to stop once it gets started. Make sure that your arms remain slightly bent during the 'quick, quick' in order to remain close to your partner and be ready for a new lead."

Student Success Goal

- Two consecutive repetitions of the row step, to music.

To Decrease Difficulty

- Isolate each part without a partner.

To Increase Difficulty

- Do more than two consecutive row steps.
- Experiment with another variation immediately before and after the row step. For example, try a half-rotation turn or a wrap and an unwrap.

8. Double Cross

Purpose and Organization

- This drill introduces another variation option that is also a transition from a two-hands joined position into a one-hand joined position.
- For a total of six counts, use the cues "face side, center, slide" to correspond to "slow, slow, ball-change," respectively.

Instructions to Class

- "The double cross is a variation that starts in a two-hands joined position and

ends in a one-hand joined position—with your right hands joined! Thus, it is not possible to do consecutive repetitions of the double cross.

The following are the direction changes.

a. Lift both arms to form two arches. Make a quarter turn CCW to face the outside. Without releasing hands, bring your own left hand behind your head (see Figure 3.8a).

b. Release your left hands, keep your right arms straight, and make a quarter turn CW to face your partner (see Figure 3.8b).

c. Release your right hands, and slide your arms down to grasp right hands (see Figure 3.8c)."

- "Regardless of the tempo of the music, you may either take one step with each direction change (to face side, then face partner) or keep your feet together and accent the direction changes by rotating your shoulders very sharply."

- "As you and your partner feel more comfortable with the direction changes involved in the double cross, experiment with the speed of your actions. Ultimately, time your actions to fit within a total of six counts."

- "Because you end up in a right-hand to right-hand position, the leader may lead immediately into a brush step at the end of the row step."

Student Success Goal

- Demonstrate a fluid sequence combining the double cross with a brush step, to music.

To Decrease Difficulty

- Add either one or two positions prior to bringing the arms behind the heads, giving each new position two counts (see Figures 3.9a and b). This slows down the timing to yield either a 10-count, double-cross step (use cues "lift, turn, lower, face partner, ball-change") or an 8-count double cross step (use cues "lift and turn, lower, face partner, ball-change").

To Increase Difficulty

- Add at least two repetitions of the row step prior to the double-cross and brush variations.

a Face left side   b Face partner   c Ball, change

Figure 3.8 Six-count double cross step (two counts per position).

a Lift arms (two counts)

b Turn left (two counts)

Figure 3.9   To decrease difficulty, add more positions prior to the six-count double cross step.

9. *Natural Combinations*

Purpose and Organization

- This drill highlights four-lead combinations that flow together well.
- Let the students select their own spots on the floor.

Instructions to Class

- "You may have noticed that certain variations seem to flow together more naturally. Start in a two-hands joined position with your partner and try each of the following four-lead combinations to music.

    a. A wrap, an unwrap (and release one hand), a single under, and a double under.

    b. Two half-rotation turns, two row steps, a double cross, and a brush step.

    c. Three row steps, a double cross, a brush, and a single (or double) under."

Student Success Goal

- Fluidly combine at least four variations, starting from a two-hands joined position and using proper styling, to music.

To Decrease Difficulty

- Use fewer variations in combination.

To Increase Difficulty

- Create a longer sequence that moves from a two-hands joined position to a one-hand joined position, then back to a two-hands joined position.

Drill for Swing Combination Options

10. Three-Position Combinations

Purpose and Organization

- Students may create their own sequences in this drill by connecting three partner positions.
- Let students select their own spots on the floor.
- Encourage proper floor etiquette.
- Either use chart 3.1 on page 65 to summarize the swing variations that students may combine to create sequences, or create your own handout, categorizing your selected variations.

Instructions to Class

- "Your task is to create one long sequence that both starts and ends in a semiopen position and that contains two or more variations from each of three partner positions."

Student Success Goal

- Three continuous repetitions of your selected sequence with fluidity and styling.

To Decrease Difficulty

- Shorten the length of the sequence.
- Use any number of swing basics in-between variations and transitions.

To Increase Difficulty

- Use spontaneous (instead of set) sequences.
- Rotate partners to improve lead-and-follow abilities.
- Ask either multiple couples to demonstrate at once or spotlight individual couples who are interested in performing.

Step 4 Adding Cha-Cha Variations for Longer Combinations

At this point, your students should know how to execute the basic cha-cha when in three different partner positions (a shine position, a two-hands [moving to one-hand] joined position, and a closed position) and how to demonstrate transitions to move into and out of these partner positions, creating a short sequence. Assign appropriate drills from Step 2, if your students do not have these prerequisite skills or if you want to review these skills.

By the end of this instructor step, your students should be able to

- execute at least two variations when in each of three different partner positions, and
- create spontaneous sequences that connect all three partner positions while demonstrating proper floor and partner etiquette.

PRACTICE PROCEDURES TO FACILITATE DECISION MAKING

The cha-cha drills in this step are organized according to the dance position in which they are executed and gradually build in more student choice. Use a whole-part-whole approach to present variations, and point out appropriate comparisons and contrasts. When stu-

dents have difficulty, follow the general procedures used in Step 2. As students are ready, encourage more spontaneous (instead of set) sequences that best fit the floor density (establishing a spot without bumping into others) and that complement both partners (dancing in unison instead of independently).

CHA-CHA COMBINATION OPTIONS

Chart 4.1 summarizes the cha-cha variations covered in this book and shows the interrelationship among the three dance positions (making a closed-loop cycle when connected). In addition, the options increase because these variations may be lead in any order with any number of basic steps in-between. The drills gradually connect two positions, then three positions, and add variation options from each position.

STUDENT KEYS TO SUCCESS

Watch for the following execution techniques in each drill.

- Proper dance position
- Appropriate styling
- Smooth transitions
- Fluid sequences

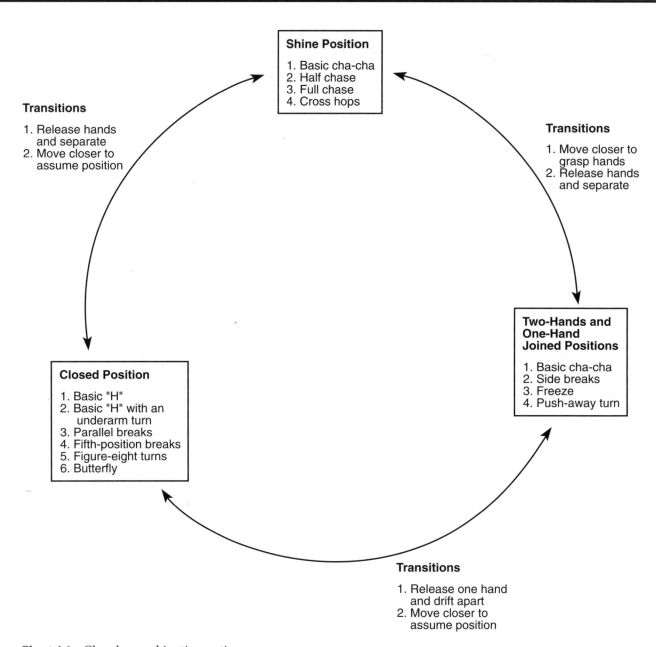

Chart 4.1   Cha-cha combination options.

Drills for Cha-Cha Variations: From a Shine Position

Note: The variations in this step are appropriate for both the American and the Latin versions of the cha-cha. Select one version or the other for all drills. As explained in Step 2, the major difference is the timing. The American version starts immediately into the forward basic for the leader while the Latin version starts with a side step, then moves into the leader's backward basic. The descriptions are the same for the forward and backward basics, once students get started. Only the timing cues will vary (i.e., 1, 2, 3-and-4 [American version], or side, 2, 3, 4-and-1; 2, 3, 4-and-1; . . . [Latin version]).

1. Full Chase

Purpose and Organization

- This drill adds another partner-challenge variation when in the shine position.
- Both parts are the same (starting on each partner's forward basic). Only the execution timing differs. The leader initiates the full chase when his left foot is free, and the follower does her backward basic until her left foot is free.
- Emphasize looking out of the corners of the eyes during the turn to give a flirtatious styling that challenges the partner to "see if you can do what I just did."

Instructions to Class

- "Another variation in the shine position is the full chase. It is very similar to the half chase except that you will end up facing your partner at the end of your forward basic (whereas you faced your partner's back in the half chase)."
- "To execute the full chase, start with a pivot turn (like you did with the half chase). Place your left foot forward, keep your right foot in the same location (feet should be in a forward-backward stride position), and pivot CW, shifting your weight onto your right foot. During the 'cha-cha-cha' portion, continue to rotate CW, making another 180-degree turn (see Figure 4.1). Try to angle your feet in the direction of the turn so that they toe in (cha), then heels travel back (cha), and back (cha). Continue into your backward basic."
- "The leader starts the full chase during his forward basic just as he did in the half chase, while the follower does her backward basic. Then, the follower does the full chase during her forward basic while the leader does his backward basic. The chase continues until the leader remains facing the follower during his forward basic."

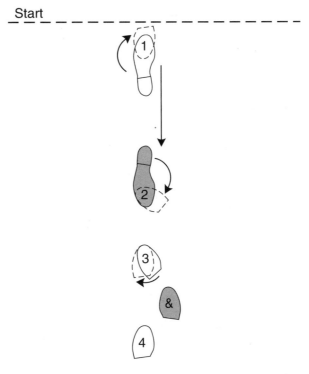

Start

Figure 4.1 Full chase on forward half of cha-cha basic (shown with American version counts; Latin version counts are 2, 3, 4-and-1).

Student Success Goal

- Competently demonstrate the full chase in each of the following ways: (a) without a partner to counts, (b) with a partner to counts, and (c) with a partner to music.

To Decrease Difficulty

- Isolate actions per counts.

To Increase Difficulty

- The leader (or either partner) may randomly initiate either the half chase or the full chase.

2. Cross Hops

Purpose and Organization

- This drill introduces another partner-challenge variation that can be executed when in a shine position and during any forward basic.

Instructions to Class

- "Either partner may challenge the other by initiating the cross hops on any forward basic, while the other partner does the backward basic. During the first 'slow,' cross your left foot over your right foot (shifting weight onto your left foot). During the second 'slow,' cross your right foot over your left foot (shifting weight onto your right foot). At the end of this second 'slow,' add a hop toward the backward direction as you insert an 'and' into the rhythm. Then, do your cha-cha-chas backward (left, right, left), and continue into your backward basic."

- "Add styling to the cross hops by extending both arms on an angle to accentuate the backward hop. Simultaneously lift your left arm and hand above shoulder-level and reach toward the back direction as you lower your right hand below your waist-level and reach toward the front direction."

Student Success Goal

- Competently demonstrate cross hops with a partner, to music.

To Decrease Difficulty

- Isolate each action within each count, without a partner.

To Increase Difficulty

- Randomly initiate any of the three shine position partner-challenge variations (half chase, full chase, or cross hops).

Drills for Cha-Cha Variations: From Two-Hands and One-Hand Joined Positions

3. Freeze

Purpose and Organization

- This drill introduces a variation that adds an extra two counts to each side break.
- Within the freeze, the extra two counts added on one side break must be added on the other side break. Otherwise, the dance will be off-phrase with the music that is grouped in measures of four beats.

Instructions to Class

- "The freeze variation is executed from a one-hand joined position and adds two counts to the side-break steps. These extra two counts must be added to both sides. The footwork on each side should be a forward-backward position with the inside foot forward. Let your body weight rock forward then backward and repeat these forward-backward weight shifts for a total of four counts (each action getting one count). Notice that these actions merely repeat your normal side-break steps twice to each side."

- "Until now, the cha-cha leads have been on a horizontal plane. For the freeze, the lead is on a vertical plane. During the leader's side break to his right side, he presses with his inside hand in a 'down-up, down-up' motion corresponding to the forward-backward strides during the 'slow, slow' counts that are repeated twice (see Figure 4.2, a and b). Then, both

Figure 4.2   The freeze rocks the weight (a) forward and (b) backward twice from a side-break position.

partners face (with shoulders parallel) and grasp both hands to continue the three quick, 'cha-cha-cha' steps while traveling sideways."

- "From the leader's left side, he repeats the freeze by lowering and raising his right hand twice while doing the four 'slow, slow' counts (or two consecutive side breaks). Then, the 'cha-cha-cha' steps travel sideways, as usual."

- "Typically, the freeze is done to each side, then another lead is given. Alternately try the freeze, then the side breaks."

Student Success Goal

- Competently demonstrate the freeze with a partner, to music.

To Decrease Difficulty

- Isolate each action with its count.

To Increase Difficulty

- Include the freeze variation within a short sequence that connects both the shine position and the two-hands joined position.

4. Push-Away Turn

Purpose and Organization

- This drill introduces a variation off the side breaks (from a one-hand joined position).

- It is very similar to the half chase, only the pivots are off the side breaks, and a quarter turn is added at the end, prior to the sideward cha-cha-chas.

Instructions to Class

- "A push-away turn may be added off the side breaks. When the leader's left foot is free to lead into a side break, he signals the push-away turn by keeping his hand horizontal (on the first 'slow') and gently pushing away the follower's

a Break   b Step   c Cha-cha-cha

Figure 4.3   Push-away turn on the leader's right side.

hand (see Figure 4.3a). Both partners make a half turn (CW for the leader and CCW for the follower) during the second 'slow' (see Figure 4.3b). Continue your turn by adding another quarter turn in order to face your partner, and grasp both hands for your sideward 'quick, quick, quick' counts (see Figure 4.3c). The push-away turn may be done on the other side as well; just reverse your actions."

- "The leader has three options as to when to lead the push-away turn. He may lead it only on one side, only on the other side, or on both sides. The follower needs to be ready to turn whenever signalled by the leader."

- "This variation may feel familiar to you because it modifies the half chase that you already know. The main differences are that the pivot starts off a side break and that there is another quarter turn

added after the pivot (to continue rotating to face your partner during the sideward 'cha-cha-cha' steps)."

Student Success Goal

- Competently demonstrate up to four consecutive push-away turns, to music.

To Decrease Difficulty

- Lead only one push-away turn using a set order, for example, on only the fourth side break.

To Increase Difficulty

- Randomly lead the freeze, the side breaks, or any of the push-away turns. Remember to execute the freeze twice to balance on both sides of the body while you may interchange the side break with the push-away turn (as long as you balance on both sides of the body).

Drills for Cha-Cha Variations: From a Closed Position

5. Basic "H" With an Underarm Turn

Purpose and Organization

- This drill uses the same footwork as the push-away turn, except only the follower turns under arched arms.

Instructions to Class

- "An underarm turn for the follower may be added off the basic 'H' pattern. At the end of the leader's left-sideward 'cha-cha-cha' steps, he lifts his left hand to form an arch. This signals the follower to do a pivot turn (half turn), moving under the arch formed by raised hands on the 'slow' (see Figure 4.4a), 'slow' (see Figure 4.4b). The leader continues the basic 'H' pattern as he shifts weight from his right onto his left foot during this 'slow, slow.' The follower continues her CW turn to face the leader, so that both can resume closed position while doing the 'cha-cha-cha' sideward steps."

Student Success Goal

- Competently demonstrate the basic "H" pattern with an underarm turn, to music.

To Decrease Difficulty

- Practice each part separately to counts.

To Increase Difficulty

- Sequence appropriate variations from a closed position and a one-hand joined position.

a Break   b Step

Figure 4.4 Underarm turn during the leader's backward break step.

6. Parallel Breaks

Purpose and Organization

- This drill introduces another variation off the basic "H" pattern when in the closed position.
- There are two parallel break options, forward and backward. Directions are defined from the leader's position (the follower's part is the reverse).
- Both partners' feet will be angled along a 45-degree angle in a parallel position during the regular break steps, with feet in a forward-backward stride position.

Instructions to Class

- "Start with the basic 'H.' The leader may substitute a parallel break position in place of the regular break steps. During the parallel break position, both partners' shoulders and feet should be parallel (angling 45 degrees) and in a forward-backward stride position."
- "To lead into a forward parallel break position, the leader slightly rotates his upper torso to face his right-front diagonal direction and steps (bringing his left foot *in front of* his right foot) along this 45-degree angle during the break steps (see Figure 4.5). Continue with sideward

cha-cha-chas to leader's left side. During the break steps on this side, he slightly rotates his upper torso to face his left-front diagonal and steps (bringing his right foot *in front of* his left foot) along this 45-degree angle."
- "As usual, on the sideward cha-cha-chas, face each other (square up). Avoid any tendencies to angle the shoulders and body on the sideward cha-cha-chas. Add the parallel break steps on both sides of the body, in place of the regular break steps."
- "To lead backward parallel breaks off the basic 'H,' the leader slightly rotates his upper torso to face his left-front diagonal direction and steps (placing his left foot *behind* his right foot) along this 45-degree angle during the break steps. Continue with sideward cha-cha-chas. During the break steps on the other side, he slightly rotates his upper torso to face his right-front diagonal direction and steps (placing his right foot *behind* his left foot) along this 45-degree angle during the break steps."

Student Success Goal

- Competently demonstrate both forward and backward parallel breaks off the basic "H," to music.

To Decrease Difficulty

- Practice each option separately. Be precise with shoulders, hips, and feet to distinguish between the facing partner position (on the sideward cha-cha-chas) and the parallel breaks (angle 45 degrees). An observer should watch the feet for a clear floor pattern.

To Increase Difficulty

- Alternate four forward-parallel breaks with four backward-parallel breaks.
- Alternate two forward-parallel breaks with two backward-parallel breaks.
- Alternate either forward or backward parallel breaks with an underarm turn off the basic "H."

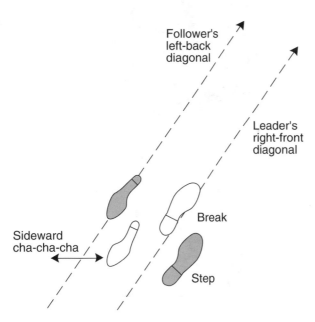

Figure 4.5   Forward-parallel break to the leader's right side.

7. Fifth-Position Breaks

Purpose and Organization

- This drill introduces another variation off the basic "H" during the break steps.
- A fifth position angles the heel of one foot beside the big toe of the other foot (from ballet).

Instructions to Class

- "Fifth-position breaks give you another variation off the basic "H" during the break steps. It is different from the parallel breaks in that the feet are positioned toe-to-heel (in a fifth position) and that both partners break backward on each side. The lead intermixes a pull of the fingers with a press of the heel of the right hand on the follower's left shoulder blade. Your left shoulder will be slightly back when your left foot breaks back, and your right shoulder will be slightly back when your right foot breaks back (see Figure 4.6)—for both partners."
- "Lead the fifth-position breaks on both sides of the body before changing leads. Use any multiple of two."

Student Success Goal

- Competently demonstrate fifth-position breaks off the basic "H," to music.

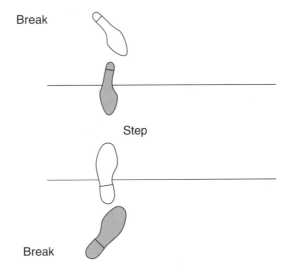

Figure 4.6 Fifth-position break to the leader's left side.

To Decrease Difficulty

- Practice without a partner to position feet properly.

To Increase Difficulty

- Release outside hands (those away from your partner) only during the fifth position breaks, keeping them curved and symmetrical, and look to each side. After any even-number repetitions, resume closed position.

8. Figure-Eight Turns

Purpose and Organization

- This drill introduces two underarm turns off the basic "H" (CW and CCW) for the woman.
- Each turn occurs during the leader's regular break steps.

Instructions to Class

- "Start in a closed position with the basic 'H.' Another variation that can be substituted during the break steps is called 'figure-eight turns.' In this variation, both the leads (arches above the follower's head) and the follower's floor pattern follow a figure-eight pattern."
- "You already know the first half of this turn: the underarm turn. For the second half maintain a one-handed position during the follower's left sideward cha-cha-chas. The leader brings his left hand across his midline and makes a small CCW circle above the follower's head as she pivots CCW during her break steps. Continue with the basic 'H.' "

Student Success Goal

- Competently demonstrate figure-eight turns off the basic "H," to music.

To Decrease Difficulty

- Do each part separately. Notice that the leaders do the basic "H" throughout, while the followers do the footwork for push-away turns on both sides (only from a different position and without her partner turning).

To Increase Difficulty

- Do four consecutive figure-eight turns.
- Alternate the underarm turn with the figure-eight turns.
- Alternate the figure-eight turns with the fifth-position breaks, using any even number of repetitions of each.
- Randomly lead the figure-eight turns, side breaks, and push-away turns.

9. Butterfly

Purpose and Organization

- This drill introduces another way to get into the side breaks, as well as a fancy variation off the basic "H" that alternates a side break with a fifth-position break.

Instructions to Class

- "Another variation off the basic 'H' is to substitute one side break and one fifth-position break during the regular break steps. Start in closed position. After a sideward break, the leader now opens his palm (with fingers pointing toward the ceiling) toward his partner. This signals the follower to match her palm to the leader's palm. Let the palms touch during the sideward cha-cha-chas, then release pressure during the break step to lead into a fifth-position break (both partners break back). This variation is called a 'butterfly' because both partners close (face each other), and open up (face the

side), like an emerging butterfly. It may be done on either side of the body."
- "To get out of the butterfly position, the leader should not present his palm to his partner and either resume closed position or lead into an underarm turn for the follower on the next side break."

Student Success Goal

- Competently demonstrate a butterfly off the basic "H," to music.

To Decrease Difficulty

- Isolate each part to counts.

To Increase Difficulty

- Alternate the butterfly with figure-eight turns.
- Alternate the butterfly with parallel breaks.
- Vary the order, and combine any three or four variations.

Drill for Cha-Cha Combination Options

10. Three-Position Combinations

Purpose and Organization

- Challenge students to execute variations from each of three positions (shine, two-hands [and one-hand] joined, or closed) to create sequences of at least four to six leads.
- Encourage proper etiquette.
- Either use Chart 4.1 on page 78 to summarize the cha-cha variations that students may combine to create sequences, or create your own handout, categorizing your selected variations.

Instructions to Class

- "Experiment with your partner to create at least four different cha-cha sequences that include at least one variation from each of three partner positions: shine position, two-hands (and one-hand) joined position, and closed position. You may use any order and any number of repetitions (following the general rule of multiples of two)."

Student Success Goal

- Competently demonstrate a sequence with at least six variations that fluidly connects three dance positions with proper styling, to music.

To Decrease Difficulty

- Demonstrate sequences that connect any two dance positions.
- Combine any four variations and connect three dance positions.
- Ask students to demonstrate only their favorite six-lead sequence.

To Increase Difficulty

- Randomly switch partners (e.g., when the music stops, connect with the closest partner that students have not already had as a partner).
- Ask for volunteers to present their sequences in a spotlight dance for the rest of the class.

Step 5　Adding Polka Variations for Longer Combinations

At this point, your students should know how to execute the polka basic in the LOD from three different partner positions (the inside-hands joined position, the semiopen position, and the closed position) and to demonstrate transitions to move into and out of these partner positions, creating a short sequence. Assign appropriate drills from Step 2, if your students do not have these prerequisite skills, or if you want to review any of these skills.

By the end of this instructor step, your students should be able to

- execute a CW turn with a partner,
- execute the basic when in a sweetheart position,
- demonstrate at least two additional transitions (from closed position to sweetheart position, then back to closed position; or from sweetheart position to inside-hands joined, then back to sweetheart position),
- demonstrate at least one variation from at least three different partner positions, and
- create spontaneous sequences that combine any six variations or transitions while demonstrating proper floor and partner etiquette.

PRACTICE PROCEDURES TO FACILITATE DECISION MAKING

Because it takes two basics before the leader's left foot (and the follower's right foot) is free

again, it is important to group at least two measures of music (four counts) together in the polka. More advanced students may be ready to phrase their basic steps by grouping in 8, 16, or 32 counts (beats of music). Use a whole-part-whole approach to present variations and transitions, and point out appropriate comparisons and contrasts. Be prepared to modify your procedures to fit different learners. As students are ready, encourage more spontaneous sequences.

POLKA COMBINATION OPTIONS

The polka variations within this step permit travel in the LOD. If another couple blocks the way, then encourage students to take smaller, more in-place steps as if marking time. Chart 5.1 lists the polka variations and transition options covered in this book. They have been categorized by the position from which they may be executed, e.g., the twist combination is done from the semiopen position. This chart provides a gestalt view, showing students both what the various options are and when to select them.

STUDENT KEYS TO SUCCESS

- Take small steps.
- Keep free hand on hip.

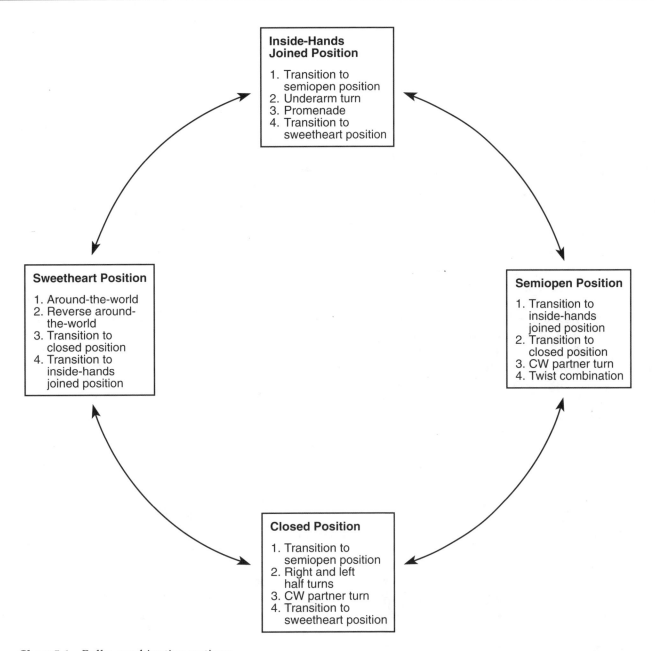

Inside-Hands Joined Position

1. Transition to semiopen position
2. Underarm turn
3. Promenade
4. Transition to sweetheart position

Semiopen Position

1. Transition to inside-hands joined position
2. Transition to closed position
3. CW partner turn
4. Twist combination

Sweetheart Position

1. Around-the-world
2. Reverse around-the-world
3. Transition to closed position
4. Transition to inside-hands joined position

Closed Position

1. Transition to semiopen position
2. Right and left half turns
3. CW partner turn
4. Transition to sweetheart position

Chart 5.1 Polka combination options.

Drills for Polka Variations: From Three Positions

1. Underarm Turn

Purpose and Organization

- This drill adds a variation from an inside-hands joined position. It emphasizes the natural swinging motion of the joined inside hands as each partner's upper torso alternately rotates slightly toward and away from each other.
- Group four polka basics together: three basics, then the follower's underarm turn

on the fourth basic. Later, the leader may use the general rule of turning the follower on the 3-and-4 counts (any second basic).

Instructions to Class

• "Group your polka basics in sets of four. Start with two regular basic steps. During the first basic, let your inside arms swing freely to the back as your shoulders rotate slightly (approximately 45 degrees) toward your partner. During the second basic, let your inside arms swing freely toward the LOD as your shoulders angle slightly away from your partner. During the third basic, again let your arms swing back as your shoulders angle toward your partner (see Figure 5.1a). During the fourth basic, the leader brings his right hand forward and lifts his hand above shoulder level (see Figure 5.1b), and makes a small, circular CW motion above her head to facilitate the follower's CW turn (see Figure 5.1c). If the follower has connected her arm with her shoulders, then her entire body (versus arm only) will turn while taking her fourth polka basic. The leader does his fourth polka basic more in place. During the turn, the leader needs to extend his fingers downward, and the follower needs to loosely cup her hand around his fingers in order to rotate freely."

Student Success Goal

• Competently demonstrate the follower's underarm turn with a partner, to music.

To Decrease Difficulty

• Isolate each partner's part.

To Increase Difficulty

• Randomly lead the underarm turn on any even-numbered basic (i.e., Counts 3-and-4).
• Add the underarm turn variation from an inside-hands joined position, transition to semiopen position, then back to inside-hands joined position.

a Counts 1-and-2   b Arm lift lead   c Counts 3-and-4

Figure 5.1   Underarm turn.

2. *Promenade*

Purpose and Organization

- This variation introduces an inside-hands joined position facing the reverse LOD that briefly moves through a two hands joined position.
- Teaching cues focusing on where partners face are helpful, using a quarter turn with each direction: "partner," "back" (reverse LOD), "partner," "forward" (LOD).
- This variation takes eight counts (or two sets of four counts).

Instructions to Class

- "To establish a tempo, start with four polka basics, letting your inside arms swing naturally. The promenade is executed within the next four polka basics (eight counts or two sets of four counts). On the first polka basic, the leader makes a CW quarter turn to face his partner (taking advantage of the natural shoulder rotation inward to face each other), extends his left hand to grasp both hands, and both partners do side, together, side steps. On the second polka basic, the leader releases his right hand, and both partners make another quarter turn to face the reverse LOD and travel backward (polka basic is now done with the new outside foot [the leader's right and follower's left]). On the third polka basic, the leader makes a CCW quarter turn to face each other again, grasps both hands, and both take side, together, side steps. On the fourth polka basic, both partners make another quarter turn to face the LOD and travel forward (this polka basic is done with the inside foot [the leader's right and follower's left]). Notice that Counts 1-and-2 are side steps, and Counts 3-and-4 alternately travel backward, then forward. Partners move inward toward each other doing two quarter turns in one direction (CW for the leader), then they move outward, away from each other doing two quarter turns in the opposite direction (CCW for the leader)."

Student Success Goal

- Competently demonstrate, with fluidity and style, the promenade with a partner, to music.

To Decrease Difficulty

- Walk through the hand changes without footwork. Move from one hand (the leader's right and follower's left) while facing the LOD, to two hands while facing each other, to one hand (the leader's left and follower's right) while facing the reverse LOD, to two hands while facing each other, and to one hand again while facing the LOD. Start with shoulders perpendicular to the LOD, and make quarter turns to be parallel with partner, perpendicular to the reverse LOD, parallel with partner, then perpendicular to the LOD again.

To Increase Difficulty

- Use any even-number repetitions of the polka basics before leading the promenade.
- Do two (or more) consecutive promenades. Either position the free hands on the hips or extend them symmetrically.

3. *CW Partner Turn*

Purpose and Organization

- This variation is one of the most popular in the polka.
- This practice sequence groups four polka basics: two in semiopen position and two to turn.
- Partners alternately remain stationary (like a post), while the other travels around and in front.
- Partners pivot at the end of Counts 2 and 4.

Instructions to Class

- "Start in a semiopen position with your partner, and do two polka basics. Firmly maintain your extended arms positions, and avoid any tendencies to lower and lift them (as was done in the swing) because lowering this extended arm is the main lead for the CW partner turn."
- "The CW partner turn takes two polka basics. The leader signals this turn by simultaneously lifting his right elbow, lowering his left arm and hand and traveling slightly in front of the follower during his first polka basic (see Figure 5.2a). The leader also places gentle pressure on his partner's left shoulder blade to signal her to take her steps in place during her first polka basic. At the end of Count 2, both partners pivot; the leader's midline sets up facing toward his original right side, then he pivots CW a half turn to face his original left side, while the follower does the reverse."
- "During the second polka basic, the leader lifts his left arm and hand higher than his shoulders and slightly lowers

his right elbow as he takes his steps in place (see Figure 5.2b). The follower travels slightly in front of the man (as he did during the first polka basic). Both pivot at the end of Count 4. To signal the end of the turn, the leader keeps his extended left arm and hand horizontal and very firm when resuming the semiopen position."

Student Success Goal

- Competently alternate two polka basics forward with a CW partner turn, to music.

To Decrease Difficulty

- Without footwork, check body positions. The arms should slant (or angle) toward the LOD. The leader's left arm moves down and his right elbow up; he then reverses them as he looks over his right shoulder and lifts his left, extended arm slightly above shoulder level.
- Isolate the footwork without a partner, using counts. The CW half-turns should occur at the end of Counts 2 and 4.

a Counts 1-and-2

b Counts 3-and-4

Figure 5.2   CW partner turn.

To Increase Difficulty

- Lead into the CW partner turn on any odd-numbered polka basic (i.e., on the leader's left foot).
- Gradually have students do two, then three, consecutive CW partner turns.

- Transition from a semiopen position to an inside-hands joined position (or vice versa), and add the CW partner turn when in the semiopen position.
- Try a CW partner turn from a closed position.

4. Twist Combination

Purpose and Organization

- This drill introduces four swivel (or twist) movements, each getting one count.
- The upper torso and arms must remain firm to provide momentum for the twists.

Instructions to Class

- "The twist combination combines four polka basics with four twist actions (each twist getting one count) for a total of 12 counts."
- "From a semiopen position, take four polka basics forward. At the end of the fourth polka basic, the leader holds his upper torso and arms (frame) very firm as he pivots on the ball of his right foot to face his partner, and crosses his left foot over his right (Count 1), while the follower does the reverse (pivots on the ball of her left foot, and crosses her right foot over her left)."
- "On Count 2, the leader pivots on the ball of his left foot and crosses his right foot over his left. On Counts 3 and 4, the

leader repeats the two previous crosses. Again, the follower does the reverse. Keep your knees slightly bent during the twists (sometimes called swivels)."

Student Success Goal

- Competently demonstrate, with fluidity and style, the twist combination, with a partner, to music.

To Decrease Difficulty

- Without a partner, place hands against a wall for support, then practice the pivot and cross steps. Notice how the upper torso remains stationary, while the lower body does all the work. Keep body weight on the balls of the feet during the twists.

To Increase Difficulty

- Do the twist combination, then lead into a CW partner turn.
- Add the twist combination within a longer combination that alternates the semiopen position and the inside-hands joined position.

5. Right and Left Half Turns

Purpose and Organization

- This drill purposely limits the right and left turns for the follower to half turns because it helps her focus on proper footwork (pivot turn techniques) and introduces spotting techniques that can help students avoid getting dizzy.

- Group four polka basics: (a) for a right half turn: two regular polka basics in closed position with two more polka basics (for the follower's turn); and (b) for a left half turn: one polka basic, two for the follower's turn, and one polka basic back to the closed position.

Instructions to Class

- "For practice, this drill uses only half turns. Both the right and left half turns for the follower groups four polka basics. However, the timing differs for each direction."

Right Half Turns

- "From a closed position, do two polka basics. At the end of the second basic, the leader signals that a right half turn is coming up by slightly rotating his frame CCW (right shoulder forward), then he lifts his left hand (to form an arch above her head). When the follower finishes her second polka basic, she keeps her weight on the ball of her left foot and pivots CW a half turn (to be under the arched arms), facing the LOD."
- "During her third polka basic, the follower looks down the LOD as she executes her polka basic (with her right foot), while the leader does his polka basic, keeping his right hand on her left shoulder blade to control the distance inbetween. At the end of this third polka basic, the leader gently presses with the heel of his right hand, and the follower pivots on the ball of her right foot a half turn CW (going under the arched arms)."
- "During the fourth polka basic, resume the closed dance position."

Left Half Turns

- "From a closed position, do one polka basic. At the end of this basic, the leader signals a left half turn is coming by rotating his frame CW (left shoulder for-

ward). Then he brings his left hand inbetween his body and his partner's body (then above her head), which facilitates the follower to execute a left half turn on the ball of her right foot (at the end of Count 2)."
- "The follower faces the LOD and executes the second polka basic with her left foot as she looks toward the LOD. At the end of this second polka basic, the follower pivots a half turn CCW on the ball of her left foot (at the end of Count 4)."
- "Both partners resume a closed position during the third and fourth polka basics."

Student Success Goal

- Competently demonstrate both right and left half turns to music.

To Decrease Difficulty

- Do each part without a partner, matching actions with the appropriate counts.
- Master right half turns before attempting left half turns.

To Increase Difficulty

- Lead a right half turn at the end of any even-numbered polka basic.
- Lead a left half turn at the end of any odd-numbered polka basic.
- Add a right half turn immediately after a CW partner turn.
- Alternately lead right half turns, then left half turns.
- Add right and left half turns within a longer combination that alternates the closed position with the semiopen position.

6. *Transitions to and From Sweetheart Position*

Purpose and Organization

- This drill introduces a new partner position and transitions to connect two different partner positions, the closed position and the inside-hands joined position.
- From a closed position, group four polka basics to transition into the sweetheart position, and group either two or four

polka basics to transition back to the closed position.
- From an inside-hands joined position, group either two or four polka basics into a sweetheart position, and group either two or four polka basics back to an inside-hands joined position.

Instructions to Class

From a Closed Position to a Sweetheart Position

- "The transition to sweetheart position from a closed position (see Figure 5.3a) takes four polka basics. Do a regular right half turn on Counts 1-and-2 (see Figure 5.3b). On Counts 3-and-4, as the follower faces the leader, he transfers her hand from his left to his right hand (see Figure 5.3c). Then he continues with a small, CW circular motion above her head to signal a third half turn into the sweetheart position (see Figure 5.3d) with both partners facing the LOD (with the follower a half-step in front of and to the right side of the leader). Both do a fourth polka basic in this position."

- "At the end of any Counts 3-and-4, the leader may lead a left half turn and transfer the follower's right hand from his right hand back to his left hand and into the closed position."

From an Inside-Hands Joined Position to a Sweetheart Position

- "The transition to sweetheart position from an inside-hands joined position takes either two or four polka basics. At the end of an underarm turn, the leader places his partner's left hand into his left hand and grasps her right hand (at shoulder level)."

- "On any odd-numbered basic, the leader may resume an inside-hands joined position. He releases his right hand, circles his left hand over the follower's head to lead a CCW turn, then transfers his partner's left hand to his right hand."

Student Success Goals

- Competently demonstrate transitions from a closed position to a sweetheart position, and back to a closed position, to music.
- Competently demonstrate transitions from an inside-hands joined position to a sweetheart position, and back to an inside-hands joined position, to music.

To Decrease Difficulty

- Practice the leads without footwork. Make sure that the hand changes are done in-between the bodies (to hide them).

To Increase Difficulty

- From a closed position, add the transition into sweetheart position immediately after a CW partner turn.

a Closed position   b Counts 1-and-2, first half turn   c Counts 3-and-4, second half turn   d Sweetheart position, third half turn

Figure 5.3 Polka transition from the closed to the sweetheart position.

Drills for Polka Variations: From a Sweetheart Position

7. Around-the-World

Purpose and Organization

- This drill introduces a variation from the sweetheart position that brings the follower CW around the leader.
- Group four polka basics to set up, then four polka basics to execute this variation.

Instructions to Class

- "From the sweetheart position, the leader may initiate an around-the-world variation (he is the world, and the follower moves around him). There are four polka basics to set up, and four polka basics to execute this variation. Do not let go of your partner's hands throughout this variation."
- "Do three polka basics from the sweetheart position. On the fourth polka basic, the man brings his right hand down and his left hand over the woman's head for a right half turn (she is facing the reverse LOD) (see Figure 5.4a)."
- "The leader continues his left hand over his own head during the first polka basic. On the second polka basic, he brings his right hand behind his own head, as his left hand gently pulls the follower to his left side (see Figure 5.4b)."
- "On the third polka basic, the leader gently pulls his left hand in front of his body (see Figure 5.4c) and brings his right hand over his own head, then over the woman's head, to lead a turn into the sweetheart position again (see Figure 5.4d)."

Student Success Goal

- Competently demonstrate the around-the-world variation with a partner, to music.

a Fourth polka basic   b Sixth polka basic   c Seventh polka basic   d Eighth polka basic

Figure 5.4 Around-the-world executed within eight polka basics from a sweetheart position.

To Decrease Difficulty

- Practice the arm leads without any footwork.
- The leader needs to take small steps and move a bit to one side or the other to decrease the distance that the follower has to travel around him.

To Increase Difficulty

- Add the around-the-world variation within a longer combination, alternating the sweetheart position with the closed position.

8. Reverse Around-the-World

Purpose and Organization

- This drill introduces a variation from the sweetheart position that brings the follower CCW around the leader.
- Group four polka basics to set up, then four polka basics to execute this variation.

Instructions to Class

- "The reverse around-the-world brings the follower CCW around the leader. Again, do not let go of your partner's hands."

- "Do four polka basics in sweetheart position. To lead the reverse around-the-world variation, the leader brings his right hand over his partner's head on the first basic (see Figure 5.5a) and over his own head to lead his partner to his left side (see Figure 5.5b) on the second basic. On the third polka basic, he continues to pull his right hand horizontally to his right side, bringing his left hand both over his own head and his partner's head (see Figure 5.5c), then on the fourth polka basic, he turns his right hand in a small

a First polka basic   b Second polka basic   c Third polka basic

Figure 5.5   Reverse around-the-world.

CCW circle to complete the follower's left turn back into the sweetheart position."

Student Success Goal

- Competently demonstrate the reverse around-the-world variation with a partner, to music.

To Decrease Difficulty

- Practice the arm leads without any footwork.
- The leader needs to take small steps and move a bit to one side or the other to decrease the distance that the follower has to travel around him.

To Increase Difficulty

- Randomly alternate four basics to set up, then lead either the around-the-world or the reverse around-the-world.
- Add the reverse around-the-world variation within a longer combination, alternating the sweetheart position with either the closed position or the inside-hands joined position.

Drill for Polka Combination Options

9. Spontaneous Sequences

Purpose and Organization

- The purpose of this drill is to review all variations learned so far, to encourage students to create longer sequences that combine any six or more variations or transitions (connecting three or four partner positions), and to demonstrate proper floor etiquette.
- Either use chart 5.1 on page 89 to summarize the polka variations that students may combine to create sequences, or create your own handout, categorizing your selected variations.

Instructions to Class

- "Politely ask a partner to dance. Assume you are on a dance floor. The leaders will need to select the appropriate polka variation for the traffic encountered. If another couple is immediately in front of you, take smaller steps, marking time. If no couples are immediately in front, then you may travel. Create one long sequence that includes at least one variation from at least three different dance positions."

Student Success Goal

- Create spontaneous sequences, with fluidity and style, that combine any six variations or transitions, to music.

To Decrease Difficulty

- Use a set order.
- Gradually lengthen sequences.

To Increase Difficulty

- Do fewer basics in-between.
- Create sequences that combine four dance positions.
- Ask for volunteers to spotlight dance for others to watch.

Step 6 Adding Fox-Trot Variations for Longer Combinations

At this point, your students should know how to execute the basic fox-trot rhythms (box and magic) when in a closed dance position, to demonstrate two variations (a left-box turn and half-box progressions [backward half-box progression was practiced in reverse LOD]), and to create a short sequence involving at least four leads. Assign appropriate drills from Step 2, if your students do not have these prerequisite skills, or if you want to review any of these skills.

By the end of this instructor step, your students should be able to

- demonstrate both stationary and traveling variations,
- execute the backward half-box progression while traveling in LOD, and
- create spontaneous sequences that combine at least six different variations (intermixing box and rhythm variations) while demonstrating proper floor and partner etiquette.

PRACTICE PROCEDURES TO FACILITATE DECISION MAKING

Use a whole-part-whole approach when introducing new variations, and categorize information to give students an idea of how everything fits together. Slowly move students from closed-practice situations (same tempo, same order when combining variations, and same defined space available) to open-practice situations (different tempos; a variety of orders, or a random order, when combining variations; and constantly changing space [which occurs when multiple couples dance in LOD on the dance floor]).

FOX-TROT COMBINATION OPTIONS

One way of categorizing information to help students both move information from short-term memory into long-term memory and recall from long-term memory is based on how the variations are used when on a dance floor. Two general categories are used in this book: Maintain a stationary position (if other couples block forward movement), or travel in the LOD (if other couples do not block forward movement). These categories reflect an open situation (because the amount of available space and the number of couples vary). To be most successful on the dance floor, your students need to practice the situations that they will later encounter. Thus, all of the variations in this step are categorized according to whether they are executed from a stationary position (stationary variations) or if they permit travel in the LOD (traveling variations). As students are ready, encourage more spontaneous sequences that best fit the floor traffic. Chart 6.1 summarizes the fox-trot variations covered in this book according to their purpose on the dance floor.

STUDENT KEYS TO SUCCESS

Watch for the following execution techniques in each drill.

- Keep upper torso and head erect.
- Maintain frame (arm connection with partner).
- Both partners look over the other's right shoulder when in a closed position.
- A longer stride on the "slow" as compared to the "quick" rhythms.
- Side steps no wider than shoulder-width.
- Maintain a constant distance from partner.

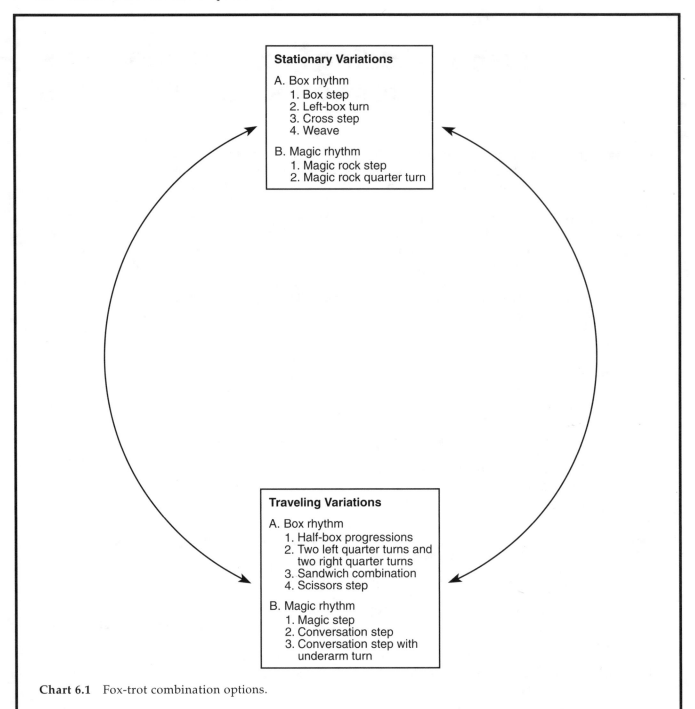

Stationary Variations

A. Box rhythm
    1. Box step
    2. Left-box turn
    3. Cross step
    4. Weave

B. Magic rhythm
    1. Magic rock step
    2. Magic rock quarter turn

Traveling Variations

A. Box rhythm
    1. Half-box progressions
    2. Two left quarter turns and
       two right quarter turns
    3. Sandwich combination
    4. Scissors step

B. Magic rhythm
    1. Magic step
    2. Conversation step
    3. Conversation step with
       underarm turn

Chart 6.1 Fox-trot combination options.

Drills for Fox-Trot Variations

1. Magic Rock

Purpose and Organization

- This is a stationary variation from a closed dance position. It is helpful whenever students need to maintain their location or to move to the leader's left (and around another couple).

- Start all leaders facing the same direction, then use the LOD. The follower's part is the reverse of the leader's part.
- Either give students a two or four repetition limit of the magic rock because it progresses them sideways, or ask them to experiment and discover for themselves just how many repetitions are most useful.

Instructions to Class

- "The magic rock is a stationary variation that is very useful when another couple abruptly appears in front of you and your partner—halting forward progress. The magic rock step uses the magic rhythm (SSQQ) within six counts (or 1-1/2 measures of music)."
- "The leader holds his right palm firmly (at the end of the first 'slow') to signal no more forward motion (see Figure 6.1a). On the second 'slow,' the leader gently pulls his right hand toward his midline and rocks his weight back onto his right foot (see Figure 6.1b). Try this without, then with a partner; keep your feet in a forward-backward stride position in order to emphasize the rocking motion."

- "Add the regular side, close actions during the 'quick' (see Figure 6.1c), 'quick' (see Figure 6.1d) cues. The leader may gently press with the heel of his right hand to signal the sideward movement."

Student Success Goal

- Competently demonstrate the magic rock without a partner to counts, then with a partner to music.

To Decrease Difficulty

- Isolate counts with actions. On the side, close, make sure that the steps are to the side versus on a diagonal.

To Increase Difficulty

- Alternate the magic rock (a stationary variation) with the magic step (a traveling variation), using any even-numbered repetitions of each. How many repetitions of each work best? (Students will discover that fewer repetitions of the magic rock [e.g., two or four] are most effective for the purpose of maneuvering around another couple. Additional repetitions progress them sideways [cutting through the center of the room instead of staying along the perimeter of the room and in the LOD].)

a Magic rock forward on Counts 1,2

b Magic rock backward on Counts 3,4

c Side step on Count 5

d Close feet on Count 6

Figure 6.1 Magic rock footwork and counts.

2. *Magic Rock Quarter Turn*

Purpose and Organization

- The magic rock quarter turn is a stationary variation that has the advantage of rotating CCW (similar to the left-box turn).
- Start students in closed position, and use the four walls of the room for orientation. When students are ready to practice in the LOD, orientate the leaders to face in four directions: the LOD, the center of the circle, the reverse LOD, and the outside of the circle (back toward center of circle).

Instructions to Class

- "The magic rock quarter turn is comparable to the left-box turn because they both use four quarter turns to get back to the original front. This variation helps you maintain a stationary location until the traffic ahead of you and your partner clears."
- "The only difference between the magic rock and the magic rock quarter turn is the quarter turn during the second 'slow.' To facilitate the turn, the leader rotates his upper torso CCW and angles his right toe inward, while the follower rotates her upper torso CCW and angles her left toe

outward. Both step along a diagonal and end up facing a new wall. An extra styling action may be added at the end of the second 'slow' (on Count 4), as both partners brush their free foot alongside their pivot foot prior to the side step, which sharpens the quarter turn."
- "On the 'quick, quick' (Counts 5 and 6), do your normal side, close steps (see Figure 6.2, a and b)."
- "Repeat this process three more times until you end up back where you started. The momentum for the quarter turn comes from rotating the shoulders and upper torso CCW at the end of the first 'slow' and from maintaining elbow contact with your partner."

Student Success Goal

- Competently demonstrate four magic rock quarter turns without a partner to counts, then with a partner to music.

To Decrease Difficulty

- Isolate footwork on each count. Experiment with a slight knee bend to use the full two counts for the "slow" counts.
- Alternately do two magic rock steps, then one magic rock quarter turn. Repeat fac-

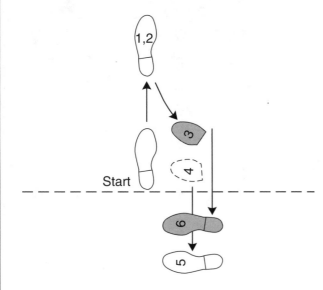

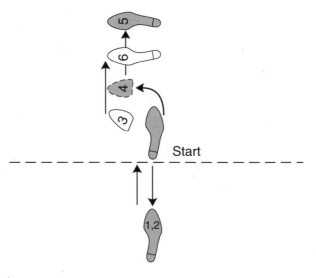

a   b

Figure 6.2   Magic rock quarter-turn footwork and counts (a) for the leader, and (b) for the follower.

ing a new wall, until back to the original front.

- Face the LOD; alternately do magic steps along the length of the room, then do a magic rock quarter turn to square the corner. Do magic steps along the width of the room, then do a magic rock quarter turn to square the corner. Repeat. (This modification uses the four walls of the

room to get students orientated to travel around the perimeter of the room.)

To Increase Difficulty

- Alternately do two magic rock steps, then four magic rock quarter turns.
- Combine any two fox-trot variations with four magic rock quarter turns: for example, two box steps, four magic steps, and four magic rock quarter turns.

3. Two Left Quarter Turns and Two Right Quarter Turns

Purpose and Organization

- This drill introduces a second traveling variation using the box rhythm.
- Travel the length of the room, then in the LOD.

Instructions to Class

- "Whenever you have the open space to travel, the preferred option is to select a traveling variation. The combination of two quarter turns left and two quarter turns right gives you another box rhythm option (besides the half-box progressions) that travels in the LOD."
- "From a closed position, do two left box quarter turns (eight counts) to end up with the leader facing reverse LOD. Now, the leader has two options: either continue CCW to complete a left box turn (if forward motion is blocked), or reverse directions to do two right (CW) quarter turns (if forward motion is possible). To do the second option, the leader gently pulls the palm of his right hand toward his midline and rotates his upper torso and frame CW approximately 45 degrees, which facilitates a toe-in position with his left foot (in his left, back, diagonal direction). He brings his right foot briefly beside his left foot at the end of 'slow,' while making a quarter turn, then continues with his side, close ('quick, quick,' or Counts 3, 4). On his second quarter turn to the right (CW), the CW shoulder rotation facilitates a toe-out position with his right foot (in his right, front, diago-

nal direction). He continues with the rest of the box quarter turn (see Figure 6.3a)."
- "The follower does the reverse (see Figure 6.3b). After two left quarter turns, she rotates CW with a toe-out position with her right foot (along her right, front, diagonal direction). The remaining touch, side, close occurs on Counts 2, 3, 4. The second right quarter turn is executed with a toe-in position with her left foot (along her left, back, diagonal direction), and she finishes the box quarter turn."
- "If you find that you are traveling more laterally than forward, check that your shoulders are perpendicular to the diagonals and that your reaching step is taken on the diagonals (either toe-in or toe-out, on each Count 1). A typical error is to rotate beyond 45 degrees, which modifies this traveling variation to a stationary variation."

Student Success Goal

- Competently demonstrate two left quarter turns and two right quarter turns without a partner to counts, then with a partner to music.

To Decrease Difficulty

- Clearly indicate the diagonals (45-degree angles) that permit forward travel. For those students who cannot visualize the appropriate 45-degree angle, consider placing tape, yarn, or string on the floor, and remember to remove the tape at the end of class.

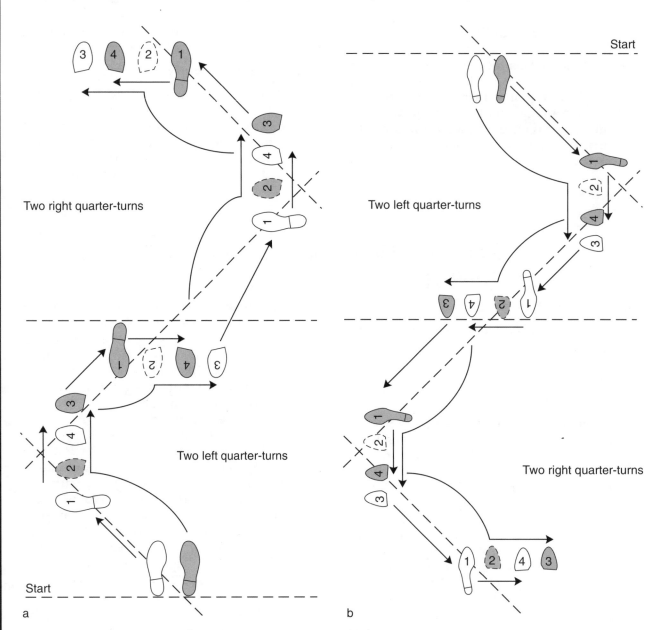

Figure 6.3   Combination of two left quarter-turns and two right quarter-turns (a) for the leader, and (b) for the follower.

- Use the image of opening a door (as you rotate two quarter turns CCW) and shutting it (as you rotate two quarter turns CW).

To Increase Difficulty

- Try consecutive repetitions.
- Combine any other fox-trot variation with this one.

4. *Sandwich Combination*

Purpose and Organization

- This combination adds backward half-box progressions to the previous variation, which now gives students the option of using the backward half-box progressions to travel in the LOD.

- Whenever the leader travels backward in the LOD, he needs to look over one shoulder to ensure that the traffic flow permits forward motion.
- If the leader notices while going into the two left quarter turns that the forward motion is blocked, then he has to make some quick decisions. He may decide to leave out the backward half-box progressions and combine the two quarter turns left with the two quarter turns right, or he may decide to continue with a left-box turn.

Instructions to Class

- "You know how to do the backward half-box progressions in the reverse LOD. Now that you know how to combine the two left quarter turns and the two right quarter turns, you can add the backward half-box progressions in-between these quarter turns (like adding meat between two slices of sandwich bread). This 'sandwich' combination permits travel in the LOD (see Figure 6.4, a and b)."

- "After leading two left quarter turns, assume that the LOD is open. The leader may now gently pull his right palm and fingers toward his midline to signal that he will be traveling backward. Execute at least two half-box progressions backward (starting with his left foot). After any even-numbered repetitions of the backward half-box progressions, the leader may rotate his shoulders CW as he toes-in with his left foot to lead into the two right quarter turns."
- "Whenever the leader has his back toward the LOD, he needs to look over his left shoulder to survey the floor traffic. The follower may help alert the man (verbally or nonverbally) that there is another couple immediately in their path. If there is not enough space to travel in the LOD, then the next option is to do two left quarter turns (to maintain location, if another couple is in the way)."

Student Success Goal

- Competently demonstrate the "sand-

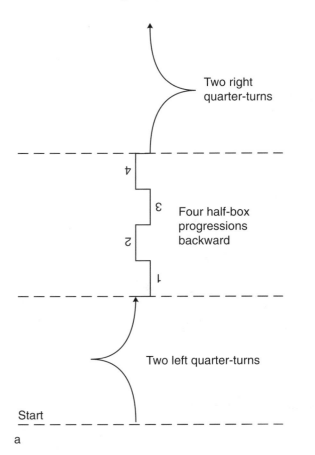

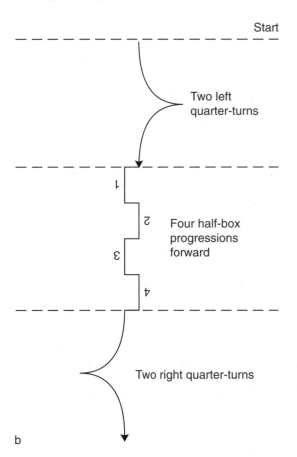

Figure 6.4 The sandwich combination option adds half-box progressions backwards (a) for the leader, and (b) for the follower.

wich" combination without a partner to counts, then with a partner to music.

To Decrease Difficulty

- Do four or more (instead of two) repetitions of the half-box progressions backward (to allow more time to think about the next lead).
- Isolate and practice each option separately. For example, after two left quarter turns, (a) continue with two right quarter turns, (b) continue with two left quarter turns, or (c) lead any even-num-

bered repetitions of the half-box progressions backward. After backward half-box progressions, either (a) continue with the two right quarter turns, or (b) continue with two left quarter turns.

To Increase Difficulty

- Ask the leaders to randomly lead the sandwich option and to use their best judgment as to which variations are most appropriate for the floor traffic.
- Substitute backward magic steps for the backward half-box progressions.

5. Cross Step

Purpose and Organization

- The cross step is a stationary variation that uses box rhythm.
- This variation requires lower and upper body isolation. One way to practice the swivel and body isolation is to ask students to face a wall, place their hands on it for support, transfer their weight onto the balls of their feet, and swivel both heels one way and their toes the other (like on a twisting exercise platform).

Instructions to Class

- "The cross step is a fancy stationary variation that is fun to do. The cross step starts with a forward half box. However, at the end of your side step, swivel on the ball of your foot (the leader's right and follower's left) to face a 45-degree angle (the arms remain in closed position, yet lower body and shoulders have rotated approximately 45 degrees to face the extended arms). On the second 'quick,' step on your outside foot (the leader's left and follower's right). On the 'slow,' cross your inside foot (the leader's right and follower's left) over the other, and swivel on the ball of that foot to face your partner again. Do the side, close in closed position (see Figure 6.5, a and b)."
- "Any number of repetitions of the cross step may be lead. However, if there are

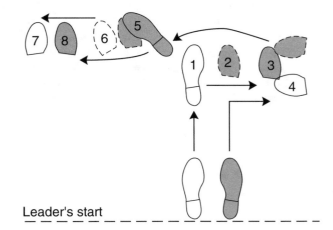

Leader's start

a

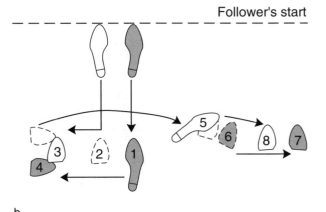

Follower's start

b

Figure 6.5   Cross step footwork and counts.

multiple, consecutive repetitions, you will travel toward the center of the room (instead of remaining stationary or traveling, which are the more desired options)."

Student Success Goal

- Competently demonstrate the cross step without a partner to counts, then with a partner to music.

To Decrease Difficulty

- Practice swivels on balls of feet with hands placed against a wall for support. Notice that only the lower body rotates, which the arms remain in place.

- Alternate two box steps with two cross steps (using a set order).

To Increase Difficulty

- Combine the cross step with at least one other variation, such as:

  a. Two box steps, then two cross steps (two stationary variations)
  b. Two (or four) half-box progressions forward, then two cross steps (a traveling and a stationary variation)
  c. Two left quarter turns and two right quarter turns, then two cross steps (a traveling and a stationary variation)

6. Weave Step

Purpose and Organization

- The weave is a stationary variation that also uses box rhythm, and it is a modification of the cross step. The weave step takes four sets of four counts (equivalent to a half box with three consecutive crosses, alternating sides).
- The weave step introduces an open (side-by-side) position as the hands of the extended arms are released when facing each side. Arms need to be symmetrical and curved, so that the elbows are in front of the shoulders (i.e., they can be seen in the student's peripheral vision).

Instructions to Class

- "The weave step is a modification of the cross step that starts with a forward half box and adds three consecutive cross steps. At the end of the forward half box, the leader releases his left hand grasp as he presses the follower's left shoulder blade with the heel of his right hand, to face the side (see Figure 6.6a). Keep your arms curved and symmetrical on the first cross step (see Figure 6.6b). If the follower keeps her arms curved and extended, the leader may easily place the

heel of his left hand on her back during the 'quick, quick' counts in order to rotate and open the arms to the other side. Do the second cross step (see Figure 6.6c) with the other foot (the leader's left and follower's right). Then, the leader presses again with the heel of his right hand on the 'quick, quick' counts to rotate to the other side. Do the third cross step (same as the first cross step); regrasp hands (see Figure 6.6d), and resume a closed dance position on the side, close steps."
- "An additional styling point is to look to the side that you open up toward."

Student Success Goal

- Competently demonstrate the weave step without a partner to counts, then with a partner to music.

To Decrease Difficulty

- Try the arm positions to each side without the footwork. Then, merge both footwork and arm positions using the box rhythm.

To Increase Difficulty

- Combine the weave step with any other fox-trot variation. Ask students to discover which other variations work best with the weave step. (At first, it may seem difficult to do the cross step immediately before or after the weave step.

The difference is whether the leader stays within the closed position or releases his grasp to open to the sides.)

a Open position to leader's left side

b Cross inside feet, and open arms on second half of box

c Cross inside feet, and open arms on third half of box

d Cross inside feet, and regrasp hands on fourth half of box

Figure 6.6 Weave step.

7. *Conversation Step*

Purpose and Organization

- This drill introduces a traveling variation that uses magic rhythm.
- The conversation step uses two positions: closed and semiopen.

Instructions to Class

- "The 'conversation' step is ideal for talking with your partner. It uses magic rhythm, starts in a closed position, and is a traveling variation. Take the regular 'slow, slow' steps forward. Then the leader presses with the finger of his right hand to rotate his partner a quarter turn CCW as he rotates a quarter turn CW. The 'quick, quick' steps are taken sideways toward the LOD. The leader alternates the forward 'slows' in a semiopen position toward the LOD, with the side, close steps facing each other in a closed position."

- "To lead out of the conversation step, the leader arcs his right arm to bring the follower a half turn CCW prior to the 'quick, quick' counts as he remains facing the LOD. Then, both do the side, close steps in closed dance position."

Student Success Goal

- Competently demonstrate the conversation step without a partner to counts, then with a partner to music.

To Decrease Difficulty

- From a semiopen position, check that the shoulders alternately are perpendicular to the LOD (on "slow, slow"), then parallel with LOD when facing inward (on "quick, quick").

To Increase Difficulty

- From a semiopen position on the "slow, slow" portion, the leader may lead a CW

underarm turn for the woman. She steps forward in the LOD on her right foot, pivots on the second "slow" (when the leader lifts his left arm and gently presses on her left shoulder) to face the reverse LOD with her left foot back, and continues another quarter CW turn to face her partner to do the side, close.
- Combine any variation with the conversation step.

- Set up for the conversation step using magic rock turns: Do a magic rock quarter turn, a magic rock half turn (the leader faces outside of circle—use momentum to increase the amount of turn, then do the side, close). Press with the heel of the right hand into the semiopen position, and continue the conversation step.

8. Scissors Step

Purpose and Organization

- The scissors step is a traveling variation that uses box rhythm.
- This variation brings both partners' right sides, then their left sides, together as they follow a zig-zag floor path.

Instructions to Class

- "The scissors step starts in closed position. At the end of a forward half box, the leader presses with his right-hand fingertips to bring the woman on his right side as he angles CCW to his left-front diagonal direction, and she angles CCW to face her left, back diagonal direction. From this setup position, half box steps are taken along each diagonal, making a zig-zag floor path progressing in the LOD."
- "Pivot 90 degrees on each 'quick, quick' to face the diagonal. Figure 6.7a shows the setup prior to the third half box toward the leader's right-forward diagonal direction."

Leader pivots 90 degrees CCW towards his left-front diagonal on quick, quick

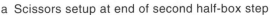

a Scissors setup at end of second half-box step   b Reach on slow of third half-box step

Figure 6.7   The setup and reach for the leader's right-front diagonal direction.

- "It is important to have either both right shoulders and hips or both left shoulders and hips toward each other. The general rule for executing the scissors step is to take the long, reaching step on the 'slow' with the leg closest to the LOD, or the opposite leg from the intended diagonal direction. For example, the leader steps on his right foot toward his left-front diagonal on the second half box, pivots CW 90 degrees on the quick, quick steps to face his right-front diagonal, then steps with his left foot toward his right-front diagonal (see Figure 6.7b) on the third half box. The follower steps with her left foot toward her right-back diagonal on the second half box, pivots 90 degrees CW on the quick, quick steps, then steps with her right foot toward her left-back diagonal on the third half box. Both take the 'quick, quick' counts to rotate toward the next diagonal."
- "To come out of the scissors step, the leader only rotates to face the LOD (instead of continuing past the LOD toward the diagonal) during any even-numbered half box (after his right foot steps toward his left-front diagonal). He must firmly keep his shoulders perpendicular to the LOD instead of letting them rotate past the LOD."

Student Success Goal

- Competently demonstrate the scissors step without a partner to counts, then with a partner to music.

To Decrease Difficulty

- Without footwork, orient the diagonal directions with a partner, then try the footwork without a partner.

To Increase Difficulty

- The leader may come out of the scissors step (anytime after his right foot steps toward his left diagonal) by lifting his left hand (at the end of the "slow") to signal a CW underarm turn for the follower, then gently pressing with the heel of the right hand to facilitate her turn (on the "quick, quick") and resume a closed position facing the LOD.

Drills for Fox-Trot Combination Options

9. Combining Four Stationary Variations

Purpose and Organization

- The purpose of this drill is to encourage students to combine at least four stationary variations.
- Use the LOD, and ask students to observe how the stationary variations keep them within a confined space.

Instructions to Class

- "Assume that you are dancing on a very crowded dance floor with so many couples that you cannot travel in the LOD. In this case, the leader's best option is to lead a stationary variation. For practice, combine at least four stationary variations from those known so far: there are four box rhythm variations (box step, left-box turn, cross step, and weave), and two magic rhythm variations (magic rock and magic rock quarter turn) to choose from."

Student Success Goal

- Competently combine, with fluidity and style, any four stationary variations, to music.

To Decrease Difficulty

- Combine any two, then any three stationary variations.

To Increase Difficulty

- Create four or more sequences that combine four stationary variations (varying the order and the number of repetitions of each).

10. Combining Four Traveling Variations

Purpose and Organization

- The purpose of this drill is to encourage students to combine at least four traveling variations.
- Use the LOD, and ask students to observe how the traveling variations progress them forward in the LOD.

Instructions to Class

- "Imagine that you and your partner are now on a dance floor that is not crowded—there is plenty of space to travel in the LOD. In this case, the leader's best option is to lead a traveling variation. For practice, combine at least four traveling variations from those known so far: there are four box rhythm variations (half-box progressions forward, two left quarter turns and two right quarter turns, sandwich combination, and scissors step), and four magic rhythm variations (magic step forward, magic step backward, conversation step, and conversation step with an underarm turn) to choose from."

Student Success Goal

- Competently combine, with fluidity and style, four traveling variations, to music.

To Decrease Difficulty

- Combine any two, then three traveling variations.

To Increase Difficulty

- Create four or more sequences that combine four traveling variations (varying the order and the number of repetitions of each).

11. Mixing Stationary and Traveling Variations

Purpose and Organization

- The purpose of this drill is to review all variations learned so far, to encourage students to intermix stationary and traveling variations, and to encourage floor-appropriate sequences.
- Encourage students to demonstrate proper floor and partner etiquette.
- Either use Chart 6.1 on page 100 to summarize the fox-trot variations that students may combine to create sequences, or create your own handout, categorizing your selected variations.

Instructions to Class

- "The most realistic dance floor situation requires that the leader select the most appropriate variation for the floor traffic encountered. He may choose a stationary variation (when the forward path is blocked) or a traveling variation (when the forward path is unblocked). It takes a lot of practice to be able to create spontaneous sequences."

Student Success Goal

- Create spontaneous sequences of six or more variations that best fit the floor traffic.

To Decrease Difficulty

- Do more than two repetitions of each variation.
- Mix any five variations.

To Increase Difficulty

- Do fewer repetitions of each variation.
- Ask volunteers to demonstrate their sequences for others to watch.

Step 7   Adding Waltz Variations for Longer Combinations

At this point, your students should know how to execute the basic waltz from a closed position, to demonstrate two variations—a left-box turn and half-box progressions (the backward half-box progression was practiced in reverse LOD)—and to create a short sequence involving at least four leads. Assign appropriate drills from Step 2, if your students do not have these prerequisite skills, or if you want to review any of these skills. Notice that many of the same box rhythm variations may be used within both the waltz and the fox-trot, except that the timing differs (the waltz gets three beats per measure while the fox-trot gets four beats per measure).

By the end of this instructor step, your students should be able to

- demonstrate both stationary and traveling variations,
- execute the backward half-box progression in the LOD, and
- create spontaneous sequences that combine at least six different variations while demonstrating proper floor and partner etiquette.

PRACTICE PROCEDURES TO FACILITATE DECISION MAKING

Because it takes two half boxes before the leader's left foot (and the follower's right foot) is free again, it is important to group at least two measures of music (six counts) together in the waltz and, ideally, to use phrases (grouping 24 counts of music). You may cue a phrase in the waltz for your students by counting either four sets of six counts (**1**-2-3-4-5-6, **2**-2-3-4-5-6, **3**-2-3-4-5-6, **4**-2-3-4-5-6) or eight sets of three counts (**1**-2-3, **2**-2-3, **3**-2-3, **4**-2-3, **5**-2-3, **6**-2-3, **7**-2-3, **8**-2-3).

WALTZ COMBINATION OPTIONS

The variations within the LOD dances (waltz, polka, and fox-trot) may be categorized according to whether there is space available. If no other couples block forward progress in the LOD, then encourage your students to select any of the traveling variations. If another couple abruptly blocks forward progress, then encourage your students to select any of the stationary variations. These two categories of variations help students make quicker decisions and help them better understand how to combine variations to create spontaneous sequences. Chart 7.1 lists the waltz variations and options covered in this book.

STUDENT KEYS TO SUCCESS

Watch for the following execution techniques and styling in each drill.

- Keep upper torso and head erect.
- Maintain frame (arm connection with partner).
- Both partners look over the other's right shoulder when in closed position.
- Feet offset (versus toe-to-toe) when in closed position.
- Touch the floor with the heel first on Count 1 and with the ball of the foot first on Counts 2, 3.
- Let the body lower slightly on Count 1, rise on Count 2, and start to lower on Count 3.
- Side steps no wider than shoulder width.
- Maintain a sustained flow of movements.
- Curve arms (keep the elbows in front of the shoulders).

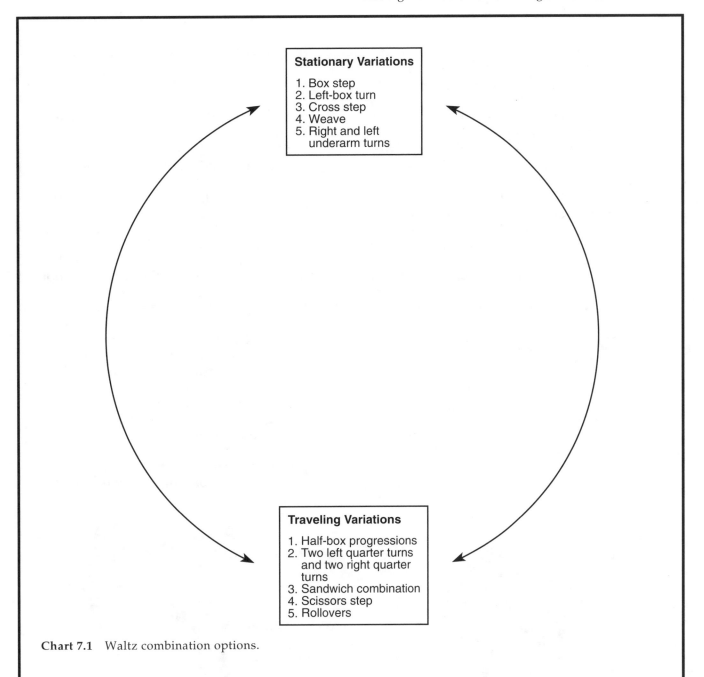

Stationary Variations

1. Box step
2. Left-box turn
3. Cross step
4. Weave
5. Right and left underarm turns

Traveling Variations

1. Half-box progressions
2. Two left quarter turns and two right quarter turns
3. Sandwich combination
4. Scissors step
5. Rollovers

Chart 7.1   Waltz combination options.

Drills for Waltz Variations

1. Right and Left Underarm Turns

Purpose and Organization

- This drill introduces a turn for the follower either off the forward half-box progression or the box step.
- The general execution rule for the follower's turn (when she is traveling backward in the LOD) is to pivot on the ball of the foot opposite the direction of the turn, i.e., if weight is on the ball of the right foot, turn left; or if weight is on the ball of the left foot, turn right. In each case, she takes her regular long

stride on Counts 1 and 4, except she keeps her heel off the floor when the lead is given so that she can pivot at the end.

- The general leading rule is to signal a left turn when the leader's left foot is free (to begin another half box) or a right turn when the leader's right foot is free (to begin another half box).
- Watch the followers for any tendencies to let the elbows move behind the shoulders on a right turn or across the body on a left turn (this is called "spaghetti arms"). She needs to connect her arm to her shoulders (keeping her right elbow approximately 45 degrees in front of her right shoulder) and keep the shoulders connected to her arms so that her entire body turns, not just the right arm.

Instructions to Class

- "An underarm turn may be added either to the box step (stationary variation) or to the forward half-box progressions (traveling variation). The right (CW) turn (see Figure 7.1, a and b) is sometimes referred to as an outside turn (away from the leader's midline), while a left (CCW) turn (see Figure 7.2, a and b) is some-

times referred to as an inside turn (across the leader's midline). Start the lead on the downbeat (either Count 1 or Count 4) by lifting the left arm to form an arch (for a right turn) or by bringing the left hand across the leader's midline (for a left turn), and assisting the follower's turn (right hand heel press on the right turn or continuing a CCW circle above her head on the left turn) during the leader's side, close steps."

- "When the follower receives the lead as she takes her long, reaching step on the downbeat, it signals her to not place that heel down. Staying on the ball of the foot permits her to pivot at the end of the backward reaching strides (Counts 1 and 4). Then the turn is executed on the remaining two counts (making two weight changes—one on each count). The general execution rule for the follower's turn is to pivot on the foot opposite the direction of the turn, i.e., pivot on the ball of the right foot to turn left or pivot on the ball of the left foot to turn right. Keep feet parallel in a forward-backward stride position during the turn. Keeping the weight on the ball of the pivot foot fa-

a Follower's left foot reaches on count 4 (keep weight on ball)

b CW turn on Counts 5, 6

Figure 7.1 A waltz right turn occurs on the second half-box progression.

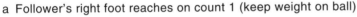

a Follower's right foot reaches on count 1 (keep weight on ball)

b CCW turn on Counts 2, 3

Figure 7.2   A waltz left turn occurs on the first half-box progression.

cilitates the follower's turn (permitting a half turn, instead of a quarter turn)."

- "With the box step, lead a *left* underarm turn when the leader's *left* foot is executing a forward half box, and lead a *right* underarm turn when the leader's *right* foot is executing a backward half box."
- "With the forward half-box progressions, lead a left underarm turn when the leader's left foot is executing a forward half box, and lead a right underarm turn when the leader's right foot is executing a forward half box."
- "During the turn, both partners should avoid a tight grip. One option is to open the hands and gently press fingers (downward for the leader and upward for the follower). Both partners need to keep their elbows curved. The follower needs to avoid any tendency to push her right hand toward the ceiling and to straighten her right elbow, which means that she is leading the turn. Another option that works well for the left turn is for the leader to extend a finger (or two)

downward and let the follower loosely cup her hand around his fingers."

Student Success Goal

- Competently demonstrate both the right and left underarm turns without a partner, to counts, then with a partner, to music.

To Decrease Difficulty

- Isolate each partner's role by specific count.
- Practice only one turn direction at a time.
- Use a set pattern, for example, do two half boxes (or a waltz box step), then a left underarm turn, and a fourth half box; or do three half boxes, then a right underarm turn.

To Increase Difficulty

- Alternately lead the left underarm turn, then the right underarm turn.
- Vary both the order and the number of basics in-between the underarm turns.

2. Two Left Quarter Turns and Two Right Quarter Turns

Purpose and Organization

- This drill introduces a second traveling variation.

Instructions to Class

- "Whenever you have the open space to travel, you can now choose either forward half-box progressions or a new combination of two left quarter turns and

two right quarter turns (see Figure 7.3, a and b)."

- "From a closed position, do two left box quarter turns (six counts) with the leader facing the reverse LOD. Again, the leader has two choices: either continue CCW to complete a left box turn, or reverse directions and do two right (CW) quarter turns. To lead this second choice, the

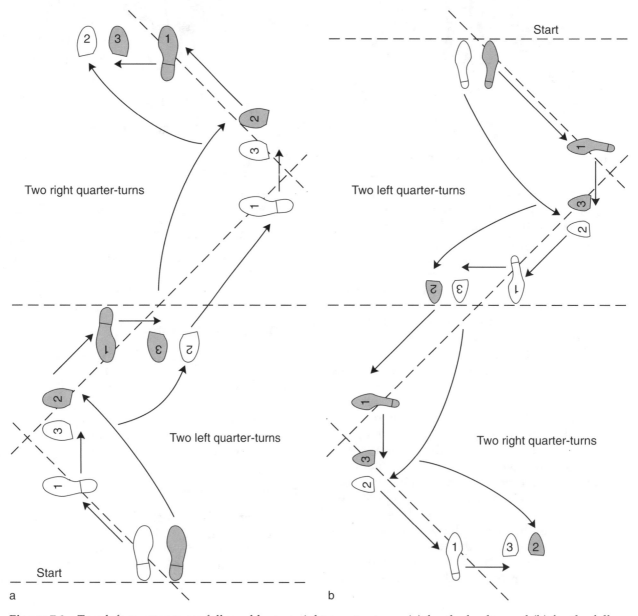

Figure 7.3 Two left quarter-turns followed by two right quarter-turns (a) for the leader, and (b) for the follower.

leader gently pulls the palm of his right hand toward his midline and rotates his upper torso and shoulders CW approximately 45 degrees. This rotation facilitates both a toe-in position with his left foot and a right quarter turn. Do the regular side, close steps facing the center of the circle. On the leader's second right quarter turn, the CW shoulder rotation facilitates a toe-out position with his right foot. He finishes the side, close steps while facing the original front (LOD)."

- "The follower's part is the reverse, so that the CW rotation facilitates a right foot, toe-out position, then a left foot, toe-in position on the first count of each right quarter turn, respectively."

- "Both partners need to watch that they are stepping along the diagonals. If you find that you are not progressing forward, then you are rotating your body beyond 45 degrees."

Student Success Goal

- Competently combine two left quarter turns and two right quarter turns without a partner, to counts, then with a partner, to music.

To Decrease Difficulty

- Clearly mark the diagonals on the floor.
- Use the image of opening a door (as you rotate CCW) and shutting it (as you rotate CW).

To Increase Difficulty

- Lead consecutive repetitions of two left quarter turns and two right quarter turns.
- Practice both traveling options and both options after two left quarter turns.

3. Sandwich Combination

Purpose and Organization

- This drill shows students how to execute the backward half-box progressions while traveling in the LOD.
- There are potential hazards when the leader has his back to the LOD. He needs to look over one shoulder and be certain that there are no other couples in the way.

Instructions to Class

- "The backward half-box progressions can easily be placed between the two left quarter turns and the two right quarter turns (like adding meat between two slices of sandwich bread). This addition combines three variations that travel forward in the LOD (see Figure 7.4, a and b)."

- "Start in closed dance position with your partner. Take two left quarter turns (the leader is facing the reverse LOD after six counts). At this point, the leader has three options: (1) continue into a left box turn, if there is no room to travel; (2) reverse into two right quarter turns, if there is room to travel; and (3) travel backward in the LOD with any even-numbered repetitions of half-box progressions, then continue to travel in the LOD with two right quarter turns, if there is room to travel."

- "The lead for option three is to keep the shoulders perpendicular to the LOD as the leader gently pulls his right palm toward his midline and steps backward with his left foot to begin the half-box progressions backward. For practice, do four backward half-box progressions. The leader needs to look over his left shoulder to make sure that no other couples are in the way."

- "To lead out of the backward half-box progressions, do the normal leads for two right quarter turns, i.e., rotate upper torso 45 degrees CW and toe-in with the left foot. Avoid any tendency to overrotate, which will result in lateral movement instead of forward traveling."

Student Success Goal

- Competently demonstrate the "sandwich" combination without a partner to counts, then with a partner to music.

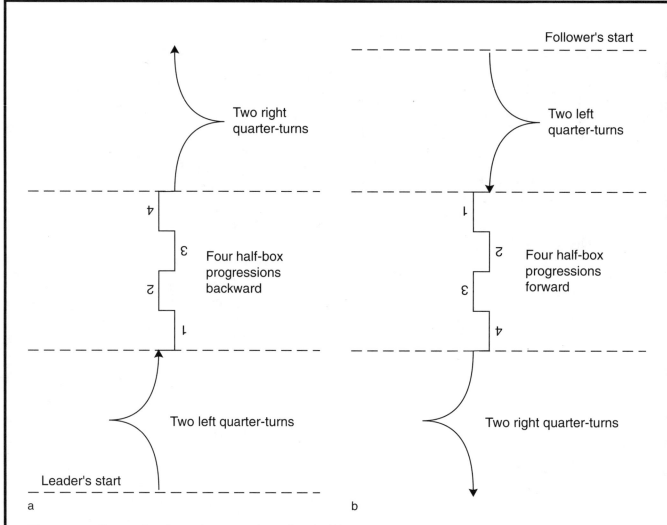

Figure 7.4 The sandwich combination places four half-box progressions in between two quarter-turns.

To Decrease Difficulty

- Use a set order (e.g., repeat each variation at least twice, with more repetitions, to give more time to think ahead) to practice each option.

To Increase Difficulty

- Use a random order to practice each option.

4. Cross Step

Purpose and Organization

- The cross step is a stationary variation that requires lower- and upper-body isolation because the arms and shoulders remain stationary while the feet and hips swivel to the side.

Instructions to Class

- "You may have noticed within the box step and the half-box progressions that the direction for the first half of the box is always executed in a forward direction, while the second half occurs either in the backward direction or in the forward direction, respectively. Another direction that you have not used yet is to the side. The cross step is a fancy, stationary variation that moves to the side on the second half of the box step (see Figure 7.5, a and b)."

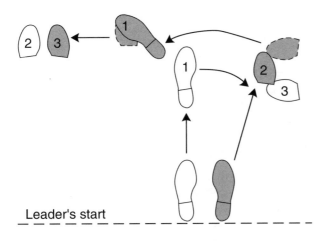

Leader's start

a

Follower's start

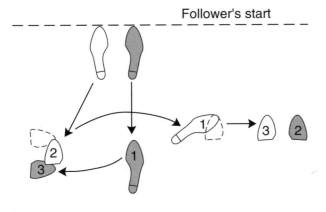

b

Figure 7.5   Cross step footwork and counts.

• "Start in closed dance position with your partner. Start the first half of a box step, except add a swivel (on Count 2) to face the side (the leader's left and the follower's right) on the close step (Count 3). Keep your upper body in the proper frame, and let your lower body do the twisting."
• "On Count 1 of the second half box, cross your inside foot (the leader's right foot and the follower's left foot) over the other foot. Twist back to face your partner and take your side step (on Count 2). On Count 3, close feet."
• "Because the cross step travels to the side, it is a good choice to move left, around another couple. Notice that multiple cross steps cut across the center of the circle, which is not a desired option."

Student Success Goal

• Competently demonstrate the cross step without a partner to counts, then with a partner to music.

To Decrease Difficulty

• Practice the swivels on the balls of the feet by placing the hands against a wall for support.
• Use a set order (for example, alternate two box steps with two cross steps).

To Increase Difficulty

• Both partners may add styling by looking toward the extended arms when executing the cross portion.
• Combine the cross step with at least one other variation. Suggested combinations follow.

    a. Two (or four) half-box progressions forward and two cross steps
    b. A left-box turn and two cross steps
    c. Two left quarter turns and two right quarter turns, and two cross steps

• Reduce the number of repetitions of in-between variations.

5. Weave

Purpose and Organization

• The weave is a stationary variation and a modification of the cross step.
• The weave introduces an open position (side-by-side position) as the hands of the extended arms are released when facing each side. Arms need to be symmetrical and curved with the elbows in front of the shoulders. (Review these positions, as shown in Figure 6.6, a-d, for the foxtrot.)

Instructions to Class

• "The weave modifies the cross step because it starts with a forward half box and adds three consecutive cross steps for a total of 12 counts (two sets of six counts). Start as if leading the cross step, then release the left hand and keep the right hand on the follower's back while both face the leader's left side. Do the cross step in this open position. The follower needs to keep her elbows curved so that the leader can easily place his left hand on her right shoulder blade to facilitate the cross step on the opposite side (second cross step). Then, he places his right hand on the follower's left shoulder blade to signal a third cross step (to the leader's left side again). Resume a closed dance position at the end of the third cross step."

- "Adding styling to the weave by looking to the side that you open up toward. Slightly bend your knees on each cross step to maintain rise and fall."

Student Success Goal

- Competently demonstrate the weave without a partner to counts, then with a partner to music.

To Decrease Difficulty

- Try the arm movements to each side without footwork. Try the footwork without the arms. Then, merge them using a slow count.

To Increase Difficulty

- Combine the weave with any other waltz variation.

6. Scissors Step

Purpose and Organization

- The scissors step is a traveling variation that follows a zig-zag floor path. (Review Figure 6.7, a and b, for the fox-trot.)
- It starts in a closed dance position.

Instructions to Class

- "The scissors step is a traveling variation that follows a zig-zag floor path. It starts in a closed position. At the end of a forward half box, the leader gently pulls with the fingers of his right hand to face his left-front diagonal, keeping the follower positioned ahead of him with right shoulders and hips toward each other."
- "The general rule for executing the scissors is to take the long, reaching step with the leg closest to the LOD, or the opposite leg from the diagonal direction (e.g., the leader's right foot when traveling toward his left-front diagonal or the follower's left foot when traveling toward her right-back diagonal). During the 'quick, quick,' both partners pivot a quarter turn to face the other diagonal direction."
- "Anytime that the leader's right foot is free, he may come out of the scissors step by pivoting only an eighth of a turn to face the LOD again. He must keep his shoulders perpendicular to the LOD and firmly keep his closed dance position (once momentum is established, it tends to keep going)."

Student Success Goal

- Competently demonstrate the scissors without a partner to counts, then with a partner to music.

To Decrease Difficulty

- Make sure that the diagonals are followed (instead of rotating beyond the diagonals, which would modify this variation to be a stationary one).

To Increase Difficulty

- Lead a right underarm turn to come out of the scissors.
- Use a modified two-hand position (extend arms to sides at shoulder level) during the scissors.
- Use a modified two-hand position during the scissors and alternately lead right, then left, underarm turns.

7. Rollovers

Purpose and Organization

- The rollovers travel in the LOD.
- This variation starts in a closed position, then modifies a semiopen position to an open position by releasing hands as in the weave, except now facing the LOD. Rollovers result when the partner on the inside (left side) rolls in front of and across the other to the outside (right side), while the other partner does the basic in place.
- It typically takes six half-box basics (grouping three counts) to execute the rollovers.

Instructions to Class

- "Start in a closed position. During the first basic, lead into a semiopen position (the leader on the left, the follower on the right) facing the LOD. On the second basic, the leader rolls (turns CW) across to the right side as the follower does her basic in place. On the third basic, the follower rolls across as the leader remains in place. On the fourth basic, the leader again rolls across while the follower remains in place. On the fifth basic, the leader maintains contact as the follower moves in front of the leader and back into closed position. The sixth basic is a forward half-box progression. It helps to travel along a diagonal whenever you roll across your partner."

Student Success Goal

- Competently demonstrate the rollovers without a partner to counts, then with a partner to music.

To Decrease Difficulty

- Modify this variation by not releasing hands. This gives the leader more control. Now this variation moves from a closed to a semiopen position, then back to a closed position (without releasing hands, allowing a cross step that is executed while facing the LOD).
- Lightly maintain arm contact as arms slide apart and hands open toward the LOD. Use a triangle image to interconnect students with the LOD and each other.

To Increase Difficulty

- Combine the rollovers with any other waltz variation.
- Vary the number of consecutive rollovers with the leader's option to bring the follower back to closed position whenever she rolls across.

Drills for Waltz Combination Options

8. Combining Four Stationary Variations

Purpose and Organization

- The purpose of this drill is to encourage students to combine at least four stationary variations.
- Use the LOD, and ask the students to notice how the stationary variations do not progress.

Instructions to Class

- "Assume you are dancing on a very crowded dance floor. In this case, the best option is to lead variations that do not progress in the LOD. It takes practice to quickly modify your movements in order to avoid collisions with other couples."

Student Success Goal

- Competently combine, with fluidity and style, any four stationary variations.

To Decrease Difficulty

- Combine any two, then any three, stationary variations.

To Increase Difficulty

- Create four or more different sequences that combine four stationary variations (varying the order and the number of repetitions).

9. *Combining Four Traveling Variations*

Purpose and Organization

- This drill encourages students to combine at least four traveling variations.
- Use the LOD, and ask students to be aware of how much distance they cover in the LOD (especially as compared to the stationary variations).

Instructions to Class

- "Imagine that you are now on a dance floor that is not crowded—there is plenty of open space to travel in the LOD. In this case, the best option is to lead traveling variations."

Student Success Goal

- Competently combine, with fluidity and style, four traveling variations, to music.

To Decrease Difficulty

- Combine any two, then any three, traveling variations.

To Increase Difficulty

- Create four or more different sequences that combine four traveling variations (varying the order and the number of repetitions).

10. *Mixing Stationary and Traveling Variations*

Purpose and Organization

- The purpose of this drill is to review all variations learned so far, to encourage students to intermix both stationary and traveling variations, and to encourage floor-appropriate sequences.
- Either use chart 7.1 on page 113 to summarize the waltz variations that students may combine to create sequences, or create your own list.

Instructions to Class

- "The actual dance floor configurations change as the various couples move around the floor. The leader needs to select the most appropriate variation according to the floor traffic encountered.

Use this strategy to create spontaneous sequences with a partner."

Student Success Goal

- Create spontaneous sequences of six or more variations that best fit the floor traffic.

To Decrease Difficulty

- Do more than two repetitions of each variation.
- Mix any five variations.

To Increase Difficulty

- Do fewer repetitions of each variation.
- Ask volunteers to demonstrate their sequences in a "spotlight" dance.

Step 8   Expanding Your Students' Dance Options and Creativity

It is important in social dancing to work in unison with a partner to create fluid, appropriate, and continuous sequences that fit the music. This does not necessarily mean that both partners must do packaged basic steps or variations to traditional ballroom music. There are a variety of situations where partners may have a good time and politely communicate (verbally and nonverbally), without bumping into other couples, and be effective "social dancers."

You can help your students learn how to modify their current dance styles to fit (a) different styles of music, (b) different tempos, and (c) different personal goals. Survey your community to locate appropriate places to dance. Feel free to select only those drills that are most appropriate for your unique situation.

By the end of this instructor step, your students should be able to

- transfer their skills to new situations by participating in mixers,
- problem solve to create their own variations and routines, and
- demonstrate proper partner and floor etiquette.

PRACTICE PROCEDURES TO FACILITATE SOCIAL INTERACTION AND CREATIVITY

Because students often need examples of how to modify what they already know, each drill contains a sample solution and a challenge situation for students to problem solve. The true test of learning occurs when students can transfer their knowledge to a new situation. Therefore, the drills in this step will help you place students in challenge situations that they may encounter at some later date on the dance floor in their social dancing, including mixers. Because mixers include partner changes, they are fun ways to facilitate social interaction, to foster camaraderie, and to demonstrate proper etiquette. Minimal social dancing etiquette includes politely asking a partner to dance, thanking a partner for a dance, treating the partner with courtesy and respect, being a good host or hostess to help others feel welcome and comfortable, controlling movements on the floor to avoid bumping into others, and following the floor etiquette rules (i.e., stay in the outside lane for traveling, the inside lane for start or stop dances and variations, and the center area for spot and line dances).

THREE WAYS TO USE MIXERS

Mixers may be used at least three ways: as icebreakers (to facilitate interaction), as a change of pace (a new way of practicing what students already know), or as a transfer test (after students learn certain prerequisite skills). Thus, within a unit, mixers may be used as part of an orientation, as variety within the unit, or as a culminating activity. This step contains at least one mixer for each dance style covered in this book, student challenges within each drill, and suggestions for increasing or decreasing the difficulty level. Feel free to modify and select those drill situations most appropriate for you and your students' needs.

Drills for Mixers and Demonstration Routines

1. Barn Dance Mixer

Purpose and Organization

- This is a fun, introductory mixer that can be done to popular, 4/4-time music (especially current country western music). It is easy to learn.
- Any extra persons may start in-between the other couples (avoid any two singles standing side by side) because they will soon have a partner after the partner exchange.

Instructions to Class

- "Make two circles, so that the leaders are on the inside and the followers are on the outside. Pair up with a partner in a two-hands joined position. The leaders have their backs toward the center of the circle and will start with their left foot. The followers are facing toward the center of the circle and will start with their right foot."
- "The entire barn dance mixer uses 32 counts:

  a. Step side, together, side, touch (position the ball of your foot beside the other foot, without a weight change) as you travel toward the LOD, then repeat toward the reverse LOD (eight counts).
  b. Repeat a, except the followers turn CW, then CCW (eight counts).
  c. Release outside hands, hold inside hands, and both partners turn to face the LOD. Step on your outside foot, swing your inside foot across your outside foot, and kick your inside foot toward the outside. Step on your in-

  side foot, swing your outside foot across, and gently touch your outside-foot heel with your partner's outside-foot heel (four counts).
  d. Repeat c (four counts).
  e. Face your partner, walk three steps backward (using small steps), and either tap or hitch (cross and flex your foot) (four counts).
  f. Angle your body to face your left diagonal. Take three walks toward the next partner (the leaders move in the LOD, and the followers move in the reverse LOD), and touch your outside foot (four counts)."

- "Grasp your partner's hands, and repeat the dance with a new partner each time."

Student Challenge

- "How could you and your partner incorporate portions of this mixer in a short swing routine?"

Student Success Goal

- Continuous repetition of the barn dance mixer for the length of one song.

To Decrease Difficulty

- Eliminate the follower's turns.
- Do only Parts a through d.
- Use slower 4/4-time music.

To Increase Difficulty

- Modify the follower's turn to be a three-quarters turn, and do not release hand grasps during Part b.
- On Parts e and f, add a three-count turn away from, then toward, the next partner.

2. Patty-Cake Polka Mixer

Purpose and Organization

- This is a lively icebreaker.
- Use any slow polka music.

Instructions to Class

- "Make a double circle with the leaders on the inside (backs toward the center) and the followers on the outside (backs toward the outside). Hold both your partner's hands. The leaders will start with their left foot, and the followers will start with their right foot."
- "This mixer uses 36 counts.

  a. With the same foot do a heel to the side, a toe (cross foot), a heel to the side, and a toe (cross foot) (four counts).

  b. Take three slides toward the LOD, and step (change weight) (four counts).

  c. Repeat a and b with the other foot (traveling in the reverse LOD) (eight counts).

  d. Pat (or gently clap) your partner's right hand three times quickly (within two counts). Pat your partner's left hand three times quickly (within two counts). Both partners pat with both hands three times quickly (within two counts). Both partners pat their own thighs three times quickly (within two counts).

  e. Hook right elbows, and rotate first CW, then CCW, around your partner, doing four step hops each way (eight counts).

  f. Followers take four step hops toward the LOD, while the leaders take four step hops toward the reverse LOD to meet a new partner (four counts)."

- "Face this new partner, and grasp two hands to start the dance over again."

Student Challenge

- "Lead Parts a and b during a regular polka, as long as you and your partner

a   b

Figure 8.1   To increase difficulty, start from a semiopen position to do your (a) heel and (b) toe movements.

are in the inner lane (because this variation starts and stops). The outside lane needs to be open for traveling variations."

Student Success Goal

- Continuous repetition of the patty-cake polka mixer for the length of one song.

To Decrease Difficulty

- Four walking steps may be substituted for the four step hops in Parts e and f.

To Increase Difficulty

- Four triple steps may be substituted for the four step hops in Parts e and f.
- Start from a semiopen position to do your heel-toe movements (see Figure 8.1, a and b).

3. *Jesse Polka Mixer*

Purpose and Organization

- This mixer travels in the LOD and should be done in the inner lane because it alternately remains stationary, then travels.
- Use any slow polka music.
- Align students in small groups of three to six (alternating males and females, as possible).
- Designate three positions: left, center, and right (see Figure 8.2) (if the number of people is not divisible by 3, then use two per position).
- This mixer requires students to listen to your instructions so that they will know who is to move forward to the next group.

Instructions to Class

- "Stand beside your partners, face the LOD, and hook elbows. Everyone begins on the left foot. Stay in the inner lane during this mixer."

Right   Center   Left

Figure 8.2   A group of three dancers.

- "Part a uses a foot action with each count (even rhythm), while Part b uses a triple step (uneven rhythm). This mixer uses 16 total counts:

  a. Left heel-dig forward, and step (feet together). Right toe-dig behind (no weight change), and touch in place (beside left foot with no weight change). Right heel-dig forward, and step in place. Left heel-dig forward, and cross in the air (in front of your right shin) (eight counts).
  b. Starting with the left foot, do four triple steps forward (eight counts)."

- "The partner change occurs during Part b. I will call out who is to move forward to the next group: right, left, or center. If there are more than three in your group, then divide up so that either one or two partners will be moving ahead at a time."

Student Challenge

- "This variation (without a partner change) may be done by a couple."

Student Success Goal

- Continuous repetition for the length of one song.

To Decrease Difficulty

- Eliminate the partner change portion in Part b.

To Increase Difficulty

- All members add styling by slightly leaning the upper torso either backward or forward, in opposition to the direction of the heels and toes during Part a.
- During Part b, members may alternately lean slightly to the same side as their lead foot.
- Modify Part a by adding two more counts and by eliminating the partner change— you will have the 10 Step, a popular country western dance. Part a has 10 actions, each getting one count. The first four counts are the same: left heel-dig forward, and step; right toe-dig backward, and touch. Then, add a right heel-dig forward and a cross (dig the right toe in front of the left foot). Continue with a right heel-dig forward, and step; a left heel-dig forward, and cross in the air. Then do four triple steps in LOD (Part b).

4. Cha-Cha Mixer

Purpose and Organization

- Set up in a double circle with the leaders on the inside and followers on the outside. Both partners face the LOD and start with the left foot.
- Begin in a sweetheart position (review Figure 5.3d).
- Prerequisite skills for this mixer include the forward and backward cha-cha basics and the half-chase (see Step 2).

Instructions to Class

- "This Cha-Cha Mixer uses 48 counts.

  a. Start in a sweetheart position (sometimes called the Varsouvienne position, or the cape position). Both partners begin with the left foot. Do the basic cha-cha forward and backward twice (16 counts).
  b. Both partners do four half-chases while in the cape position (16 counts). Keep your sweetheart position, just reverse it when facing the reverse LOD.
  c. Both partners do two cha-cha basics traveling forward in the LOD on each step (eight counts). (Notice that this modification of the cha-cha basic requires students both to take two walks forward during the break steps and to travel with each basic.)
  d. Release hands as the leader does two more traveling basics to reach the *second* follower he passes, while his partner does two half-chases (eight counts).
  e. Repeat a through d with a new partner."

Student Challenge

- "Experiment to add at least one turn for the follower somewhere within this mixer."
- *Sample solution:* During Part c, on the second forward traveling basic, the follower could cross her right foot, then her left foot, and turn CCW on the cha-cha-cha steps. The leader can facilitate this turn by bringing his right hand over the follower's head to her left shoulder, then bringing his left hand over the follower's head to her right shoulder and releasing his left hand as he circles his right hand CCW above the woman's forehead. Resume sweetheart position after the turn.

Student Success Goal

- Continuous repetition for the length of one song.

To Decrease Difficulty

- Leave out the partner exchange in Part d, and repeat Part c twice.

- On Part d, the followers may do forward and backward basics as the leaders travel forward to the next partner.

To Increase Difficulty

- Lengthen Part a by adding another 16 counts. Cue this new Part a in eight sets of four counts (e.g., **1**, 2, cha-cha-cha; **2**, 2, cha-cha-cha; **3**, 2, cha-cha-cha; and so forth). The leader does his regular forward and backward basics eight times. At the end of the follower's fourth basic, she turns CCW during the "cha-cha-cha" portion (the leader's right hand comes over her head), and she faces her partner to do the fifth basic, except she rocks backward-forward, then turns CW back under the leader's arm during the cha-cha-cha portion (into the sweetheart position again). She repeats these turns during the cha-cha-cha portions of the sixth and seventh basics. Both partners do the eighth basic side by side (with no turn).

5. Swing Mixer

Purpose and Organization

- Start in a double circle with the leaders on the inside, and pair up partners in a semiopen position, facing the LOD.
- Prerequisite: Completion of swing drills in Step 2.

Instructions to Class

- "This swing mixer uses eight triple-lindy basics (or 48 total counts). Start in a semiopen position with your partner, facing the LOD. The leaders begin with their left foot, and the followers begin with their right foot.

  a. Do four swing basics, making a CCW quarter turn on each ball, change portion (24 counts).
  b. Do an arch-out transition (6 counts).

  c. Do an arch-in transition (6 counts).
  d. Repeat Part b (6 counts).
  e. Repeat Part c; the leader releases his partner (he stays in place) and lets her move in the reverse LOD to the next partner (she substitutes two walks for her ball, change steps) (6 counts)."

Student Challenge

- "To country western 4/4-time music, experiment to substitute two walks for the ball, change steps when executing the triple lindy, and travel in the LOD." (This is called the "Triple Two-Step" or "Double Two" in some areas.)

Student Success Goal

- Continuous repetition for the length of one song.

To Decrease Difficulty

- Eliminate the partner change.
- Use a slow tempo.

To Increase Difficulty

- Repeat this swing mixer using moderate or fast tempos.

- Lengthen the middle of the sequence, e.g., add one or more single unders or double unders (see Step 3) after Part b.

6. Waltz Mixer

Purpose and Organization

- Start in a single circle with the leaders on the left side of the followers, holding hands and facing the center. Then, a transition will be made to travel in the LOD.
- Prerequisite: Completion of waltz drills in Step 7.

Instructions to Class

- "This waltz mixer uses 54 total counts. Leaders begin with their left foot, and followers begin with their right foot.

  a. Do forward and backward half-box basics, swinging joined hands forward and backward (6 counts).
  b. Repeat Part a (6 counts).
  c. Leaders repeat Part a, while pulling the follower on his left side into a CW turn in front of him and to his right side (3 counts).
  d. Both do a backward basic (3 counts).
  e. Repeat Part c (3 counts).
  f. Leaders make a CW quarter turn to face the LOD and do their basic in place as they move into a closed position. Followers continue their CW turn to face the reverse LOD and do their basic in place as they move into a closed position (3 counts).
  g. Do two box steps (12 counts).
  h. Do three half-box progressions forward (9 counts).
  i. Add a fourth half-box progression, and slide hands down to grasp two hands with your partner (3 counts).
  j. Continue with two more half-box progressions. On the first one, the leaders

lift their left arm to form an arch for women to move under (leaders still face the LOD, and the followers still face the reverse LOD). Partners pass left shoulders as they move to meet the next partner. On the second half-box progression, all face the center in a single circle (ready to start over) (6 counts)."

Student Challenge

- "To country western 3/4-time music, select only traveling variations that progress in the LOD, and let your feet pass on each step (like walking steps without any side steps)." (This is part of the styling for the country western waltz.)

Student Success Goal

- Continuous repetition for the length of one song.

To Decrease Difficulty

- Use a slow tempo.
- Shorten the sequence, e.g., do only Parts a through d (eliminate the partner exchange), or do only Parts g through j, and resume a closed position at the end to start over again.

To Increase Difficulty

- Repeat this waltz mixer using moderate or fast tempos.
- Lengthen the middle of the sequence, e.g., after Part g, add a left-box turn (or any of the variations within Step 7).

7. Fox-Trot Mixer

Purpose and Organization

- This drill introduces a beginning and an advanced mixer.
- Both mixers start in a closed dance position, facing the LOD.
- Prerequisite for beginning mixer: box step, half-box progressions, magic step, and magic rock step (see Step 2). Prerequisite for advanced mixer: magic rock quarter turn and conversation step (see Step 6).

Instructions to Class

Beginning Mixer

- "This fox-trot mixer takes 56 total counts.

   a. Do two box steps in the LOD (16 counts).
   b. Do four half-box progressions forward (16 counts).
   c. Do two magic rock steps (12 counts).
   d. Do two magic steps with the following modifications: During the side, close steps of the first magic step, bring the follower to your right side and release hands. Both partners travel forward toward the next partner on the second magic step (leaders remain facing LOD, and followers remain facing reverse LOD). Resume a closed dance position with this new partner to begin the mixer again (12 counts)."

Advanced Mixer

- "This fox-trot mixer takes 52 total counts.

   a. Do two box steps in the LOD (16 counts).
   b. Do a magic rock quarter turn (the leader faces center) (6 counts).
   c. Do a magic rock quarter turn (the leader faces the reverse LOD) (6 counts).
   d. Do a magic rock quarter turn (the leader faces away from center) (6 counts).
   e. Do a conversation step toward the LOD on the slows, and face partner on the quicks.
   f. Repeat Part e, adding a CW underarm turn for the follower (the leader makes an arch on the first "slow," the follower turns under during the second "slow." Then, leaders cross their left foot over their right and take a large, right sideward step to match up with a new partner on their right side. The followers do the regular side, close steps (6 counts).
   g. Magic rock quarter turn (the leaders face the LOD again) (6 counts). The couples are ready to repeat the mixer with this new partner."

Student Challenge

- "To country western 4/4-time music, use only traveling magic rhythm variations, and make sure that your feet pass on each step." [The Country Western Two-Step alternates either two slows and two quicks, or two quicks and two slows. The latter version gives the advantage of matching your footwork (quicks) to the tempo of the song, then the slows are twice as long. Try both ways, and decide for yourself.]

Student Success Goal

- Continuous repetitions for the length of one song.

To Decrease Difficulty

- Eliminate the partner change.

To Increase Difficulty

- Lengthen the middle of the sequence, e.g., add a left-box turn after Part a of the beginning mixer, or add two left quarter turns and two right quarter turns after Part a of the advanced mixer (see additional fox-trot variations in Step 6).

8. Demonstration Routines

Purpose and Organization

- Use a problem-solving approach to encourage students to create their own routines for demonstration purposes, whether for other class members or for some other special event.
- Reward all participants by clapping after their performance. It takes a lot of courage (and practice) to perform for an audience.

Instructions to Class

- "You may choose whether you want to work with a partner, one or more couples, or the entire class (e.g., to create an original mixer). General guidelines follow.

   a. You'll need a specific beginning, middle, and end.
   b. Decide on the music; consider styling, accents, and themes.
   c. Connect at least two different partner positions. (If four couples are teaming together, decide what formations best fit.)
   d. Add direction changes and turns for variety and interest.
   e. Structure counts in either four sets of eight counts (32 counts within 2/4 or 4/4 music) or in four sets of six counts (24 counts within 3/4-time music).
   f. Enjoy yourself, and smile!"

Student Challenge

- "How can you modify the fox-trot variations to fit very slow, popular music?"
- *Sample solution*: Side step and touch, side step and touch, rock weight from side to side (two counts). Can rotate on rock steps.
- "Create a mixer that uses the schottische (three walks and a hop, each taking one count) using popular or folk dance music."
- *Sample solution*: Modify any of the mixers or line dances in this book.

Student Success Goal

- Create a demonstration routine.

To Decrease Difficulty

- Narrow the students' choices, giving them a choice of only two things at one time. For example, to create a group mixer, ask them the following:

   a. Do you want 4/4 or 3/4 music?
   b. Do you want to start in a double circle with a partner and facing the LOD, or facing toward the center of the circle?
   c. Which two variations (movements) do you want to combine?
   d. How can you combine these two variations to form two different rhythm patterns that you can alternate for the length of one song? Each part must be either 8 or 16 counts long (if 4/4-time music; or 6 or 12 counts, if 3/4-time music).
   e. Where could you add a partner change?

To Increase Difficulty

- Increase the length of the sequence.
- Add costumes or props.
- Perform for an audience.

Assessing Your Students' Progress

Assessments permit you to not only determine whether the goals and objectives of your social dance lesson or entire program are being accomplished, but also help you guide the ongoing teaching-learning process. The development of a fair evaluation plan to assess student achievement requires a great deal of thought on your part. Often students and teachers perceive assessment as something that occurs only at the end of a unit as a final judgment of the students' overall performance. In reality, assessment should be much more—beginning with the first class period and continuing throughout the term. Ongoing assessments keep you informed of individual and group progress and needs, and they provide guidelines for planning future lessons. In addition, students can benefit from knowing what they have mastered as well as what they need to improve. An ongoing approach to assessment, coupled with appropriate feedback, motivates students to tackle assignments instead of putting them off.

MONITORING STUDENTS' PROGRESS

You may monitor student progress through the use of formative and summative techniques. Formative assessment is an ongoing, day-by-day process that can be used within an individual lesson or class period. It involves problem-solving tasks for students, multiple appropriate student responses, and applications to real-life situations. Formative assessment enables both you and your students to identify strengths and weaknesses as they are engaged in the learning process. You can provide feedback to help students improve areas in which they are most deficient.

Summative assessment generally occurs at the completion of an instructional unit to help you evaluate students' overall strengths and weaknesses. Summative assessment typically provides a basis for establishing a grading system. It can be accomplished through objective measurements, such as knowledge and skill tests, as well as by your subjective judgment of overall student progress.

ONGOING ASSESSMENTS

It is difficult to master a number of dance styles within the short time frame of a single unit. Two special features in this book can help you provide an ongoing assessment system: (a) the Keys to Success (technique [qualitative] measures) and (b) the Success Goals (performance [quantitative] measures). This combination will provide students who have little or no experience in social dance with an opportunity to earn passing grades by developing their skills (including following the Keys to Success and applying the etiquette rules), even though they may not be accomplished dancers, as reflected in fluidity and style. An assessment system based entirely on performance outcomes (by following only the Success Goals) tends to reward the natural dancer, or those more experienced in dance, and puts added pressure on the inexperienced dancer, who feels pressured to measure up to predetermined standards of performance.

Students may have a trained partner rate their techniques, and they may record their own progress on each drill. In this book, the Keys to Success and Success Goals sections have been modified to best fit a group setting (using a competency-based approach).

In addition, each step in this book lists the student objectives to be accomplished before progressing students to the next step. The rating charts in Step 2 provide checklists, including footwork, partner orientation, and styling characteristics for eight basic dance steps. These checklists contrast beginner with accomplished dancers' responses, which you can use to categorize the skill levels within a particular class or use as a checklist for qualitative (process or technique) assessment of student progress. For very large classes, you may want to select fewer items to evaluate or modify some items to better fit the individual learners. For example, if a student has a knee problem that limits hopping, let that student leave the hop out during the polka.

Figure E.1 shows a sample evaluation form for the swing that you can use in two ways: (a) to subjectively assess students, and (b) as

7 Assessing Your Students' Progress   133

Swing Combination Options Chart*	Evaluation Criteria								
Psychomotor Skills	Footwork and execution	Rhythm and timing	Posture, position, frame	Lead and follow	Etiquette	Use of space	Variety	Fluidity and style	Overall total
A. Semiopen position variations									
1. Basic step in place									
2. Basic step moving CW									
3. Basic step moving CCW									
B. One-hand joined position variations									
1. Single under									
2. Double under									
3. Brush									
4. 1/2-rotation turn									
C. Two-hands joined position variations									
1. 1/2-rotation turn									
2. Wrap and unwrap									
3. Row step									
4. Double cross									
D. Transitions									
1. Arch-out and arch-in									
2. Roll-out and roll-in									
3. 1/2-rotation transition									
4. Release one hand during unwrap									

Key

√+ = Demonstration elements are outstanding and strong.
√ = Demonstration elements are good and clear.
√− = Demonstration elements are poor and inconsistent.
0 = Demonstration elements are negligible and unclear.

Note: Combining more than one partner position increases the difficulty, requiring longer sequences with appropriate transitions.

Figure E.1 Sample Swing Assessment Form.

a model to adapt for use with other dance styles (using the combination options charts presented in Steps 3-7). With more accomplished students, select more criteria to use for your evaluation. With beginner students, limit the number of selected criteria to no more than three or four. Figure E.1 may also be used with multiple classes to help you check off those items that you have covered in different classes and list what you plan to cover in the next class.

Much of the ongoing, day-by-day assessment can be accomplished by the students themselves. Encourage them to work in pairs or small groups to chart their progress. Quizzes and written tests at selected times throughout the unit help you assess the students' knowledge and understanding of selected concepts and definitions. Your daily observations, as well as your formal assessment should play a role in the students' final grades.

As learning is inferred from performance, there are two easy ways to measure learning: (a) Stop practicing for a few days, and observe performance (retention), and (b) have students perform in a different situation than they used for practice (transfer of knowledge). The former typically occurs whenever multiple dance styles are covered, and students are encouraged to practice outside of class. The latter can be observed through mixers that use the skills covered in a slightly different way (see Step 8 for mixer ideas). Allow practice time and an atmosphere that promotes help and encouragement.

Generally, you should let students practice under the same conditions that will prevail in the test situation. For example, in early learning stages there should be fewer variations, the same partner, the same dance position, the same tempo, the same sequence order, and fewer couples dancing at once (give other couples an assignment so that they are not watching the couples being evaluated). Later in learning, it is important for students to rapidly modify leading and following to match the demands of the situation; thus, encourage more variations, different partner positions, different partners, different tempos, multiple couples dancing at once (to adapt to the changing floor space available), and permit others to watch.

GRADING SYSTEMS

A number of different grading systems can be used for summative assessment purposes. These include letter grades, pass-fail marks, satisfactory-unsatisfactory marks, percentages, point systems, a plus-minus system, and levels of achievement (bronze, silver, or gold). Choose the system that best reflects your grading philosophy and the importance that you place on grades as part of the educational process. Whatever method you choose, it must be fair, consistent, and treat all students in a similar fashion. Your grading system should also take into account special conditions that may affect a student's final evaluation, such as illness or injury, physical handicaps, poor attendance, and cheating. To accomplish this aim, you should base the final grade on many criteria, so that no single factor—whether it be a physical test, performance outcome, class attendance, or written test—has too great a weight on a student's overall level of achievement. Let your students know your grading system during your orientation lecture. A sample overall grading scheme for a social dance unit is shown in Figure E.2. Feel free to modify it to best fit your situation (for example, you might provide a range of percentages within each category and ask students to select within the percentage range given for each category before the unit begins). Grading should not take the entire class period. Finish grading before the last week of class in order to give students feedback and to have time to dance for fun.

Sample Overall Evaluation Scheme		

Name _____ Date _____ Class _____

A final grade will be derived as follows:

Background Knowledge

Knowledge of social dance history, music structure, characteristics, and styling _____ (15%)

Physiology, Training, and Conditioning

Body alignment and carriage, posture, dance frame, and endurance _____ (5%)

Psychomotor Skills and Strategies
(per dance style covered)

Footwork and execution, rhythm and timing, use of floor space, sequence variety, fluidity of transitions, and appropriate styling _____ (50%)

Psychosocial Concepts

Nonverbal communication (leading and following), social grace and etiquette, and self-confidence _____ (30%)

Total _____ (100%)

Figure E.2   Sample Overall Grading Scheme.

Test Bank

The following questions are categorized according to rhythmic foundations, basic steps, partner positions, leading and following, and the five dance styles. Select those that best fit your needs, and modify others, as appropriate (e.g., to adjust the language level and vocabulary to match the level of the group being tested or to adjust the number of questions to match the purpose). Generally, a test of 35 to 60 questions serves most purposes (McGee & Farrow, 1987). Prepare a separate answer sheet to score the test and to evaluate performance (e.g., you may want to retain records of student performance on a particular question to evaluate whether you want to reuse that question on subsequent tests). Make sure that your answers are in random order, with no observable pattern. General instructions should inform the students to select the best answer. The answers are marked with an asterisk for the following questions.

RHYTHMIC FOUNDATIONS

_____ 1. What is one group of four beats within 4/4-time music called?
   a. meter
   b. phrase
   *c. measure
   d. rhythmic pattern

_____ 2. When the counts in a rhythmic pattern coincide with the whole beats of the music, what is this called?
   a. syncopated rhythm
   *b. even rhythm
   c. uneven rhythm
   d. underlying beat

_____ 3. What is the rate of speed of the music?
   *a. tempo
   b. beat
   c. rhythm
   d. meter

_____ 4. How many weight changes in a triple step (step, ball, change)?
   a. one
   b. two
   *c. three
   d. four

_____ 5. How many beats in a triple step (step, ball, change)?
   a. one
   *b. two
   c. three
   d. four

_____ 6. How many counts in a triple step (step, ball, change)?
   a. one and a half
   b. two
   *c. two and a half
   d. three

_____ 7. What is the rhythmic pattern for a triple step (step, ball, change)?
   a. even
   *b. uneven
   c. broken
   d. syncopated

_____ 8. What happens to the length of a step when the tempo gets slower?
   a. It gets shorter.
   *b. It gets longer.
   c. It remains the same.
   d. It varies.

_____ 9. What is the rhythmic pattern for a walk?
   a. broken
   b. uneven
   *c. even
   d. syncopated

_____10. What is the rhythmic pattern for a skip?
   a. broken
   *b. uneven
   c. even
   d. syncopated

_____11. What is the rhythmic pattern for a hop?

a. broken
b. uneven
*c. even
d. syncopated

_____12. Which basic dance step is in 2/4 time?

*a. polka
b. cha-cha
c. fox-trot
d. waltz

_____13. Which basic dance step is in 3/4 time?

a. polka
b. cha-cha
c. fox-trot
*d. waltz

_____14. What does the numerator in 4/4 time mean?

a. four accents
b. four beats
*c. four beats in one measure
d. each beat gets one count

_____15. Which dance would _not_ be executed to 4/4 time?

*a. waltz
b. cha-cha
c. fox-trot
d. swing

_____16. What does _line-of-direction_ refer to?

a. clockwise movement
*b. counterclockwise movement
c. stationary movement
d. traveling movement

_____17. What is the first count of any measure called?

a. upbeat
b. beat
c. accent
*d. downbeat

_____18. What does the 4 in 3/4-time signatures mean?

a. There are four beats per measure.
b. There are four beats per meter.
*c. Each quarter note gets one beat.
d. Each quarter note gets four beats.

_____19. In a forward walk, what part of the foot hits the floor first?

a. ball
b. toe
c. entire foot
*d. heel

_____20. In a reaching-backward walk, what part of the foot hits the floor first?

a. ball
*b. toe
c. entire foot
d. heel

_____21. When you coincide forward walks to music or counts, which of the following statements is most accurate?

a. Use a heel-ball-toe motion.
b. Use a toe-ball-heel motion.
c. The body's weight is over the heel of the working foot on each whole count.
*d. The body's weight is over the ball of the working foot on each whole count.

_____22. Which counts are accented in fox-trot and swing music?

*a. two and four
b. one and three
c. two and three
d. three and four

BASIC STEPS

_____ 1. Which basic dance step can be described as hop, step, close, step?

a. triple-lindy swing
b. fox-trot
*c. polka
d. double-lindy swing

_____ 2. In which basic dance step is the rhythm slow, quick, quick?

*a. fox-trot (box rhythm)
b. fox-trot (magic rhythm)
c. single-lindy swing
d. cha-cha

_____ 3. In which basic dance step is the rhythm slow, slow, quick, quick, slow?

a. fox-trot (box rhythm)
b. fox-trot (magic rhythm)
c. single-lindy swing
*d. cha-cha

_____ 4. Which dance has three different dance basics, according to the tempo of the music?

    a. fox-trot

    *b. swing

    c. polka

    d. waltz

_____ 5. In which basic dance step does the music accent Count 1, and there is a longer stride taken?

    a. fox-trot

    b. swing

    c. polka

    *d. waltz

_____ 6. Which dance style uses two different rhythms?

    *a. fox-trot

    b. swing

    c. polka

    d. waltz

_____ 7. Which one of the following dances is *not* executed in the LOD?

    a. fox-trot

    *b. swing

    c. polka

    d. waltz

_____ 8. Which one of the following dances is called a spot dance?

    a. fox-trot

    *b. cha-cha

    c. polka

    d. waltz

_____ 9. In which dance basic is the styling fun and flirtatious?

    a. fox-trot

    *b. cha-cha

    c. swing

    d. polka

_____ 10. In which dance basic is posture very erect with hips and shoulders aligned?

    *a. fox-trot

    b. cha-cha

    c. swing

    d. polka

PARTNER POSITIONS

_____ 1. Which dance uses a shine position?

    *a. cha-cha

    b. waltz

    c. swing

    d. fox-trot

_____ 2. Which subpart within Diagram 1 shows the semiopen position used in the swing?

    a. a

    b. b

    *c. c

    d. d

_____ 3. Which subpart within Diagram 1 shows the inside-hands joined position used in the polka?

    a. a

    b. b

    c. c

    *d. d

a   b   c   d

Diagram 1 Four partner positions.

____ 4. Which subpart within Diagram 1 shows the closed position?

    *a. a

    b. b

    c. c

    d. d

____ 5. When in the closed position, where should the feet be in relationship to your partner?

    a. They are aligned toe to toe.

    b. The leader's feet are outside of the follower's feet.

    *c. Stand a half step apart, with the right foot in-between the partner's feet.

    d. Stand side-by-side, with the feet slightly apart.

____ 6. Which base of support is most efficient in dancing?

    a. The feet are wider apart than width of the shoulders, and weight is over the whole foot.

    *b. The feet are a few inches apart, and weight is over the balls of the feet.

    c. The inside of the feet are touching, and weight is over the balls of the feet.

    d. The feet are shoulder-width apart, and weight is over the balls of the feet.

____ 7. Where is it best to look when dancing in closed position?

    a. in your partner's eyes

    b. over your partner's left shoulder

    *c. over your partner's right shoulder

    d. at the spectators

____ 8. When in closed position, approximately how high should the grasped hands be placed?

    a. level with leader's ear

    b. level with leader's shoulder

    c. level with follower's ear

    *d. level with follower's shoulder

____ 9. If you execute a fox-trot box step followed by a cross step, which two partner positions have been used?

    a. semiopen and closed

    *b. closed and semiopen

    c. shine and closed

    d. closed and open

____ 10. From what position is an arch-out led?

    a. closed

    b. open

    *c. semiopen

    d. inside-hands joined

LEADING AND FOLLOWING

____ 1. As the body weight shifts forward, which part of the body moves first?

    *a. shoulders

    b. ankles

    c. knees

    d. hips

____ 2. Another couple blocks your forward motion during the fox-trot. What is the leader's best option?

    *a. Choose any stationary dance variation.

    b. Choose any traveling dance variation.

    c. Stop.

    d. Cut across the center of the floor.

____ 3. From where does the reach of the foot begin?

    a. shoulders

    b. ankle

    c. knee

    *d. hip

____ 4. Which part of the foot hits the floor first during the backward-reaching steps for the follower?

    a. heel

    b. ball

    *c. toe

    d. entire foot

____ 5. To lead a left box turn in the waltz, the leader must

    *a. rotate shoulders and arms as a unit

    b. turn only arms

    c. use only heel or palm of hand

    d. raise left arm and hand

SWING

____ 1. Which of the following swing basics best fits slow swing music?

    a. single-lindy

    b. double-lindy

    *c. triple-lindy

    d. syncopated-lindy

_____ 2. How many beats of music are used within the swing basics?
   a. two
   b. four
   *c. six
   d. eight

_____ 3. Which of the following transitions may be used to move from a semiopen position to a one-hand joined position?
   *a. arch-out
   b. arch-in
   c. single under
   d. double under

_____ 4. Which of the following occurs during the execution of a single under?
   a. Leader remains in place throughout.
   b. Follower turns CW as partners switch locations.
   c. Leader turns immediately after the follower turns.
   *d. Follower turns CCW as partners switch locations.

_____ 5. Which of the following swing basics best fits fast swing music?
   *a. single-lindy
   b. double-lindy
   c. triple-lindy
   d. syncopated-lindy

CHA-CHA

_____ 1. How many beats of music are used within the cha-cha basic?
   a. two
   *b. four
   c. six
   d. eight

_____ 2. What type of dance is the cha-cha?
   a. LOD
   b. smooth
   *c. spot
   d. jazzy

_____ 3. From which country did the cha-cha-cha originate?
   a. Argentina
   b. Brazil
   c. Mexico
   *d. Cuba

_____ 4. When should the half-chase turn start?
   *a. on the leader's forward basic
   b. on the leader's backward basic
   c. on the follower's backward basic
   d. at any time

_____ 5. Which of the following leads might occur during a transition from the shine to the two-hands joined position?
   a. Follower travels forward on the cha-cha-chas to grasp leader's hands.
   *b. Leader travels forward on the cha-cha-chas to grasp follower's hands.
   c. Leader remains in place until follower moves close enough to grasp leader's hands.
   d. Follower remains in place throughout, with hands at sides.

FOX-TROT

_____ 1. How many counts are there in a magic rock quarter turn?
   a. two
   b. four
   *c. six
   d. eight

_____ 2. Where did the name "fox-trot" come from?
   *a. a musical comedy star's personalized styling
   b. a New England village
   c. an animal
   d. big band era

_____ 3. Who created the magic step?
   a. Harry Fox
   b. Vernon and Irene Castle
   c. Oscar Duryea
   *d. Arthur Murray

_____ 4. How many beats of music are used within two magic steps?
   a. 4
   b. 6
   c. 8
   *d. 12

_____ 5. How many beats of music are used within two fox-trot box steps?
   a. 4
   b. 8
   c. 12
   *d. 16

POLKA

_____ 1. From which country did the polka originate?
- a. England
- b. Germany
- c. Poland
- *d. All of the above

_____ 2. How many beats of music are used within the polka basic?
- *a. two
- b. four
- c. six
- d. eight

_____ 3. What type of dance is the polka?
- *a. LOD
- b. smooth
- c. spot
- d. jazzy

_____ 4. Which of the following leads might _not_ occur during a transition from the semiopen to inside-hands joined position?
- a. Leader gently pushes away with the heel of the right hand.
- *b. Leader places the right hand (that is holding the follower's left hand) on his right shoulder.
- c. Leader releases his left hand grasp.
- d. Both partners' inside hands slide down the arms of the other partner.

_____ 5. How many polka basics need to be executed before starting again with the leader's left foot and the follower's right foot?
- *a. two
- b. four
- c. six
- d. eight

WALTZ

_____ 1. How many quarter turns does a couple make in a left-box turn in the waltz?
- a. one or two
- b. two
- c. two or four
- *d. four

_____ 2. How many counts are needed to execute a left-box turn in the waltz?
- a. six
- b. nine
- *c. twelve
- d. fifteen

_____ 3. Which option would be more appropriate if someone abruptly cuts in front and blocks your forward progress?
- *a. cross step
- b. half-box progressions forward
- c. scissors step
- d. sandwich combination

_____ 4. From which European country did waltz music originate?
- a. France
- b. England
- c. Poland
- *d. Austria

_____ 5. On which beat of waltz music should the stride be lengthened?
- *a. first
- b. second
- c. third
- d. second and third

Appendix A.1
How to Use the Knowledge Structure Overview

A knowledge structure is an instructional tool. By completing one, you make a very personal statement about what you know about a subject and how that knowledge guides your teaching decisions. The knowledge structure for social dance outlined here (see Appendix A.2) has been designed for a teaching environment; it contains teaching progressions that emphasize technique and performance objectives in realistic settings.

The Knowledge Structure of Social Dance shows the first page—or an *overview*—of a completed knowledge structure. The knowledge structure is divided into broad information categories that reflect various knowledge subdisciplines. Those categories are

- background knowledge,
- physiological training and conditioning,
- psychomotor skills and strategies, and
- psychosocial concepts.

Read the knowledge structure from left to right. The background-knowledge category presents subcategories of information that represent essential background knowledge that all instructors should command when meeting their classes. Social dance background knowledge includes a brief history, the benefits and popularity of social dancing today, an introductory understanding of musical structure, and the particular dance characteristics that add style.

Physiological training and conditioning have several subcategories, including body alignment, carriage (body alignment while moving), and endurance. The participant's book has suggestions for students who want to improve their posture and carriage. You can help students warm up by slowing down the pace (and tempo) at the start and end of each class. Gradually increase the amount of continuous movement in-between in order to increase students' endurance. Because of time restrictions, these subcategories are usually the only training activities done for twice-weekly (or three times per week) classes that last approximately 50 minutes. However, in a more comprehensive teaching environment, additional subcategories should be added, including general stretching principles, injury prevention, training progressions, nutrition principles, and performance anxiety.

Under the psychomotor skills category, the presentation order for individual techniques presented in this book are as follows:

- Connecting footwork with the music (walk to music)
- Demonstrating rhythmic locomotor patterns to 4/4- and 3/4-time music, including the basic steps
- Demonstrating selected partner positions
- Adding transitions
- Adding variations

In a complete knowledge structure, each basic dance step would be broken down into those technical and biomechanical points that describe mature performance.

Once individual skills are identified and analyzed, then selected strategies (decision-making situations) are also identified and analyzed. Notice that they are arranged (from left to right) to reflect the decision-making strategies and capabilities of learners as they become more proficient. For this book, the strategies include the following:

- Follow set sequences
- Create spontaneous sequences (modified to best fit self, partner, and floor traffic)

The psychosocial category identifies selected concepts from the sport psychology and sociology literature that have been shown to contribute to the learners' understanding of, and success in, social dance. These concepts are built into the key concepts and activities presented in both the participant's book and this instructor's guide, and are as follows:

- Nonverbal communication (leading and following)
- Social grace and etiquette
- Self-confidence

In order to be a successful teacher or coach, you must convert what you have learned as a student or done as a player or performer to a form of knowing that is both conscious and appropriate for presentation to others. A knowledge structure helps you with this transition and speeds your *steps to success*. You should view a knowledge structure as the most basic level of teaching knowledge that you possess for a sport or an activity.* For more information on how to develop your own knowledge structure, see the textbook that accompanies this series, *Instructional Design for Teaching Physical Activities* (Vickers, 1990).

*Note. The hierarchical arrangement of activity-specific knowledge appeared in "The Role of Expert Knowledge Structures in an Instructional Design Model for Physical Education" by J.N. Vickers, 1983, *Journal of Teaching in Physical Education*, 2(3), pp. 25, 27. Copyright 1983 by Joan N. Vickers. Adapted by permission. The Knowledge Structure of Social Dance (Overview) on page 144 was designed specifically for the Steps to Success Activity Series by Joan N. Vickers and Judy Patterson Wright.

Appendix A.2

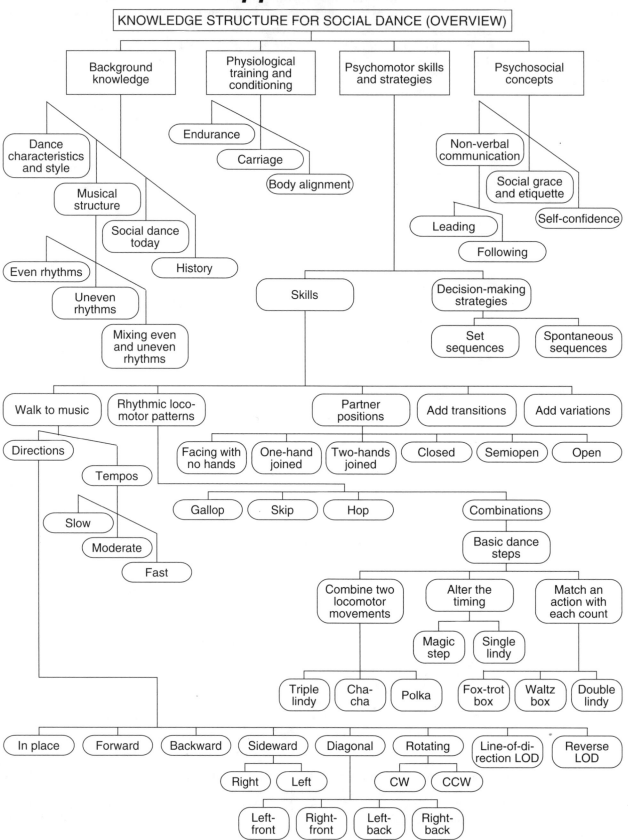

Appendix B.1
How to Use the Scope and Teaching Sequence Form

A Scope and Teaching Sequence is a master unit plan (see blank form). It lists all the learning steps to be included in your course, recorded (vertically) in the progressive sequence in which you have decided to present them and showing (horizontally) the manner and the sessions in which you teach them.

The Sample Scope and Teaching Sequence (see Appendix B.2) illustrates a completed form. This sample indicates that at the end of the sixth session, the basic steps for five dance styles have been covered (assume one to two new basics are introduced during each session). The students take responsibility for self-directed practice using proper alignment and carriage, identifying when to start with the music, and coinciding their footwork with the music. Within the test situations, or within the review sessions, you might include checklists, rating charts, or mixers.

Use the blank form to plan your daily teaching strategies. It will take some experience to predict accurately how much material you can cover during each session, but by completing a plan like this, you can compare your progress to your plan and revise the plan to better fit the next class. It will also help you tailor the amount of material to the length of time you have to teach. Be sure that your course's Scope and Teaching Sequence allots ample time for reviewing and practicing each area.

Remember that the Scope and Teaching Sequence can be affected by the number of students in a class, the collective abilities of your students, the space available, the amount of time available, and how many dance styles you wish to cover. While a completed scope and teaching sequence can serve as a guide, it is very difficult to follow it exactly. Feel free to make adjustments according to the variables mentioned.

Scope and Teaching Sequence

New [N]   Review [R]   Continue [C]   Student-directed practice [P]   Test [T]

Name of Activity _____

Level of Learner _____

Session Number ⟶

Steps	1	2	3	4	5	6	7	8	9	10	11	12	13	14	15	16	17	18	19	20	21	22	23	24	25	26	27	28	29	30

Appendix B.2

Sample Scope and Teaching Sequence

New N   Review R   Continue C   Student-directed practice P   Test T →

Name of Activity _____

Level of Learner _____

Steps / Session Number →	1	2	3	4	5	6	7	8	9	10	11	12	13	14	15	16	17	18	19	20	21	22	23	24	25	26	27	28	29	30
1 Establishing a rhythmic foundation	N	R	R	R	R	R																								
2 Introducing basic dance steps and short combinations		N	N	N	N	N	C	C	C	C	C	P	T																	
3 Adding swing variations for longer combinations														N	R	C	C	C	C	C	C	C	C	C	P	P	P	T		
4 Adding cha-cha variations for longer combinations																N	R	C	C	C	C	C	C	C	C	P	P	T		
5 Adding fox-trot variations for longer combinations																		N	R	C	C	C	C	C	C	C	P	T		
6 Adding polka variations for longer combinations																				N	R	C	C	C	C	C	C	T		
7 Adding waltz variations for longer combinations																						N	R	C	C	C	C	T		
8 Expanding your students' dance options and creativity													N					N			N							N	N	N

Appendix C.1
How to Use the Lesson Plan Form

All teachers have learned in their training that lesson plans are vital to good teaching. This is a commonly accepted axiom, but lesson plans can take many forms. You may modify the blank lesson plan to fit your needs.

An effective lesson plan sets forth the objectives to be attained or attempted during the session. If there is no objective, then there is no reason for teaching and no basis for judging whether or not the teaching is effective.

Once you have named your objectives, list specific activities that will lead to attaining each. Every activity must be described in detail—what will take place and in what order, and how the class will be organized for the optimum learning situation (see the Sample Swing Lesson Plan in Appendix C.2).

Record key words or phrases as focal points as well as brief reminders of the applicable safety precautions, e.g., to avoid bumping others.

Finally, set a time schedule that allocates a segment of the lesson for each activity to guide you in keeping to your plan. It is wise to also include in your lesson plan a list of all the music needed, as well as a reminder to check for availability and location of necessary equipment before class.

An organized, professional approach to teaching requires preparing daily lesson plans. Each lesson plan provides you with an effective overview of your intended instruction and a means to evaluate it when class is over. Having lesson plans on file allows someone else to teach in your absence.

Lesson Plan

LESSON PLAN _____ OF _____   OBJECTIVES:

ACTIVITY _____

CLASS _____

EQUIPMENT:

SKILL OR CONCEPT	LEARNING ACTIVITIES	TEACHING POINTS	TIME (MIN)

Appendix C.2: Sample Swing Lesson Plan

LESSON PLAN ___2___ OF ___30___

ACTIVITY ___Beginning swing___

CLASS ___6-7:30 p.m. Tu-Th (25 males; 25 females)___

EQUIPMENT:

1. 4/4-time popular music for mixer
2. 4/4-time slow swing music (use first selection on Side B of the soundsheet [located within the participant's book], or use Side A of the supplemental swing audiocassette [see last page of this book for more information])
3. Stereo/audiocassette player

OBJECTIVES:

1. Student reviews, practices walking mixer and partner etiquette.
2. Student is introduced to the triple step (uneven rhythm).
3. Student demonstrates triple step during mixer.
4. Student is introduced to triple-lindy swing basic (in modified, then in traditional way).
5. Student is introduced to a semiopen position.
6. Student is introduced to a rotation option while doing the triple-lindy swing basic.

SKILL OR CONCEPT	LEARNING ACTIVITIES	TEACHING POINTS	TIME (MIN)
1. Circle mixer review	• Double circle (men on inside) • Pair up partners (singles in-between) • Group 4 walks in different directions [see Drill 7, Step 1 page 22]	• Transfer body weight over ball of foot on each whole count • Encourage students to introduce themselves to a new partner • Even rhythm example (use heel-ball-toe action)	15
2. Introduce uneven rhythm	• Repeat circle mixer, only substitute 4 triple steps in each direction	• Triple step has three weight changes during Counts 1-and-2 (cues: step, ball, step) • On the "and," place ball of foot beside the heel of the working foot	10
3. Mix uneven and even rhythm	• Repeat circle mixer, only substitute 2 triple steps and 2 walks in each direction • Keep last partner.	• Men start with left foot, women with right foot • Use Counts 1-and-2, 3-and-4, 5, 6	10
4. Introduce triple-lindy basic	• All face same direction • Do basic beside partner (see Swing Drill 1, Step 2, page 33) • Repeat with fingertip pressure with partner • Repeat basic in semiopen position • Add slow swing music	• Men on left, women on right • Use triangle image • Same counts as previous, only modify 2 walks to a ball, change • Use small steps • Let torso lean on triples, remain upright on ball, change	20
5. Introduce CCW rotation option	• See Swing Drill 2, Step 2, page 36	• Start with 1/8th turns, move to 1/4 and 1/2 turns (to revolve) • Make the turn during the ball, change steps (remain in place for triples) • Gradually turn on all steps • Challenge more experienced students with a CW rotation option too	15
6. Practice two options: alternate basic in place with a CCW-rotation turn	• Students practice on own • Try with counts, then music	• Give individual feedback • Alternate partners • Practice proper etiquette	15
7. Closure	• Summarize important points, bridge to next lesson		5

References

McGee, R., & Farrow, A. (1987). *Test questions for physical education activities*. Champaign, IL: Human Kinetics.

Nygaard, G., & Boone, T. (1985). *Coaches guide to sport law*. Champaign, IL: Human Kinetics.

Vickers, J.N. (1990). *Instructional design for teaching physical activities*. Champaign, IL: Human Kinetics.

Weikart, P. (1989). *Teaching movement & dance: A sequential approach to rhythmic movement* (3rd ed.). Ypsilanti, MI: High Scope Press.

About the Author

Judy Patterson Wright and Sam Wright

Judy Patterson Wright is an accomplished dancer who has taught social dance at the junior high, high school, and college levels since 1971. She earned her PhD in 1981, her dissertation focusing on the process of learning a waltz sequence. She has taught many styles of dance, as well as physical education methods, activities, and classes in motor development and behavior.

Dr. Wright's dance experience includes a wide variety of styles—ballroom and social dance, tap dance, jazz, modern dance, ballet, folk dance, square dance, country western dance, and aerobic dancercise. Judy and her husband, Sam Wright, are popular instructors who specialize in progressive teaching methods. They have participated in country western dance competitions since 1992, dancing the two-step, waltz, cha-cha, east-coast swing, west-coast swing, and polka. As a couple they have won numer-

ous regional and national competitions, and through their company, Wright Way Productions, they have produced 12 instructional videotapes for country western dance couples.

Honored as one of the Outstanding Young Women of America in 1982, Dr. Wright has been repeatedly recognized as an Excellent Teacher at the University of Illinois at Urbana-Champaign. She has presented at the local, state, and national levels for many organizations, including two she belongs to, the American Alliance for Health, Physical Education, Recreation and Dance and the National Teachers Association for Country Western Dance Teachers.

Dr. Wright created the format for the Steps to Success Activity Series. Each book applies the latest research in an integrated manner, providing a continuum of skills and concepts sequenced to make learning easy.